Symbols:
Guiding Lights
Along the Journey of Life

A.R.E. MEMBERSHIP SERIES

SYMBOLS:
GUIDING LIGHTS ALONG THE JOURNEY OF LIFE

by Kathleen R. Prata
and the
Editors of the A.R.E.

ASSOCIATION FOR
RESEARCH AND
ENLIGHTENMENT

A.R.E. Press • Virginia Beach • Virginia

A.R.E. Press
Sixty-Eighth & Atlantic Avenue
P.O. Box 656
Virginia Beach, VA 23451-0656

Prata, Kathleen R., 1958-
    Symbols : guiding lights along the journey of life / by Kathleen
R. Prata and the editors of the A.R.E.
        p.   cm.—(A.R.E. membership series : 4)
    ISBN 0-87604-379-1
    1. Spiritual life. 2. Symbolism. 3. Symbolism (Psychology).
4. Cayce, Edgar, 1877-1945. Edgar Cayce readings. I. Cayce,
Edgar, 1877-1945. Edgar Cayce readings. II. Association for
Research and Enlightenment. III. Title. IV. Series.
BF1999.P715   1997
291.3'7—dc21   96-29938

The *A.R.E. Membership Series*

This book, *Symbols: Guiding Lights Along the Journey of Life*, is another in a continuing series of books that is published by the Association for Research and Enlightenment, Inc., for individuals who are especially interested in their personal and spiritual growth and transformation.

The A.R.E. was founded in 1931 as a nonprofit organization to study, research, and disseminate information on ESP, dreams, holistic health, meditation, and life after death. The A.R.E. continues its mission today, nurturing a worldwide membership with conferences, study groups, and a variety of publications—all aimed at helping seekers find paths that will lead to a more fulfilling life, mentally, physically, and spiritually. The hallmark of A.R.E.'s publications is to be helpful and hopeful. A.R.E. is committed to assisting in personal growth and making available nourishing entertainment.

Many of the books published by A.R.E. are available in bookstores throughout the world and all are available directly from the A.R.E.'s mail-order catalogs.

Three new books in this *A.R.E. Membership Series* are sent at no cost each year to individuals who are Sponsoring members or Life members of A.R.E. Each of the titles in this series will become available, in the year after initial publication, for purchase by individuals throughout the world who are interested in individual growth and transformation.

For more information about membership benefits of the nonprofit Association for Research and Enlightenment, Inc., please turn to the last page in this volume.

Contents

INTRODUCTION

Marla walked along the beach thinking of a creative project she was considering. It meant reaching into a new level of her work, one that would be challenging and could enhance her career. It involved working with another person who was well known in his field. He was someone she admired and whose talents she found inspiring, but she never dreamed their paths would cross. As she walked along the water's edge, she found that her ideas were endless, effortlessly leading to yet another link in her creative thought process. Marla realized that there were many possibilities that could unfold from this collaboration. At that moment, she glanced up into the sky and saw a segment of rainbow amidst a thin layer of clouds. That rainbow was symbolic confirmation that her intuitions were correct and that she needed to pursue this opportunity. She went home and wrote the man a letter describing the project she envisioned.

Signs or symbols such as Marla's rainbow are available for our interpretation each and every moment of every day. It is the way our own soul mind speaks to us, not in a language familiar to our ears, but in the language of symbols. Through symbols, your higher self communicates with you to guide you on your spiritual path. Our soul self attempts to catch our attention and prod us along on our spiritual journeys through casual conversations, songs, dreams, animals, accidents, illness, and even our "Freudian slips."

Sometimes these signs lead us directly to a new home, a new love, a new job—or whatever it is we are seeking. At other times they provide encouragement to move forward, allow the mystery of our journey to unfold, and become aligned with the Divine Plan.

Marla didn't hear a verbal command telling her what to do. The universe put a rainbow in her path on a beautiful sunny day. She interpreted this sign as a divine message that she needed to take a risk and allow the mystery of the chance meeting to unfold.

This divine guidance in the form of symbols is always available, and yet many of us fail to notice. Marla could have chosen to look the other way and dismiss the rainbow as a natural anomaly. But she didn't. She interpreted the rainbow's symbolic appearance, weighed it against her intuition and the flow of her ideas, and decided her next step was worth taking.

Denise Linn, author of *The Secret Language of Signs* says, "Everything around you, every situation you encounter, every experience you have is filled with signs regarding your life. . . If you want to discover what is occurring within the depths of your being at any given time, just look and listen to the signs around you."

Marla knew that this chance meeting was an opportunity to help her break into a higher level for her own work. The rainbow symbolized her readiness to take another step of her career ladder, and it also verified that her intuition was correct. She received an assignment to write an article about this man within hours of mailing the letter, knowing full well that it was only the beginning.

Listening to and also developing an understanding of these signs and symbols is vitally important if we want to flow with the changes not only of our daily lives, but also through the global changes that are taking place as we enter the new millennium. Take a look around you. Become aware. The signs and symbols of your life are always available, always there for notice and interpretation—a seahorse found along the shoreline, a conversation overheard while standing in the checkout line at the grocery store, dogs that appear in your dreams, a song on the radio, recurring appearances of ladybugs, or a chance meeting. These are just some of the ways that your higher self communicates with you to guide you on your spiritual path.

"The man who understands a symbol not only 'opens himself' to the objective world, but at the same time succeeds in emerging from his personal situation and reaching a comprehension of the universal . . . " says Mircea Eliade, in *The Two and the One*. "Thanks to the symbol, the individual experience is 'awoken' and translated into a spiritual act. To 'live' a symbol and correctly decipher its message implies an opening towards the Spirit and finally access to the universal."

Universal symbols are common to all humankind and are used to express our relationship to our Creator and to teach universal truths. They also tell us a great deal about our true selves.

In *Symbols and the Self*, which is richly steeped in the Edgar Cayce readings, Violet Shelley writes, "The universal symbol has been the repository of truth about the reality of the Self. Each symbol in this category is highly evocative and has many levels of significance. New insights into meaning do not invalidate the old, but they do add other levels to our understanding. The true meaning of the symbol is communicated at a level deeper than that of the intellect."

Jung believed religious symbols "give a meaning to the life of man . . . raising a man beyond mere getting and spending." Cayce, a dedicated student of the Bible, believed the Scripture held important clues to understanding universal truths. He felt that behind the literal truths stood deeper symbolic meanings.

The following is a Cayce reading explaining the *Search for God* lesson on "The Cross and the Crown":

So, He, with the cross, represents something in the experience of every entity in their activities through the earth, and has led in all of the experiences of thought in *any* of the presented forms of truth in the earth, and comes at last to the cross. So, this should be the central thought, the reason of the cross, the crown; for, as ye may be known by the name that He has given, so must the central theme, the basis of each individual's approach be: Not "What is my cross?" which is the usual first question in every *material* mind, but rather "How may I with His aid best *meet* my cross, in my approach to the crown of righteousness?" and *not* as of a temporal or even a mental kingdom, but the cross of glory, the crown of glory, in, through and by His name. (262-34)

In Cayce's dream interpretation readings, he describes three different ways that the imagery from the unconscious mind presents itself: a sign, emblem, and true symbol (or archetype).

Signs can be translated literally. Mark Thurston, author of *Dreams: Tonight's Answers for Tomorrow's Questions*, described signs as having one specific meaning for the dreamer. "A sign is often literal, lacking the richness of multiple shades of meaning found in the other two types of dream symbol," he says.

For instance when Morton Blumenthal, the stockbroker and financial backer of the Cayce work in the early years, dreamt of railroads, it most often was a literal reference to investments in railroad stock.

Emblems are highly individual and personal. They frequently appear in your dreams. Renowned Swiss psychiatrist Carl Jung believed these symbols emerged from our personal unconscious, which is shaped by our personal experiences. Dogs, for example, may have different meanings, depending upon an individual's experience. For someone who may have been bitten or attacked by a dog, dreaming of one may be a warning of an attack of some nature. For an animal lover, dogs may conjure up the image of man's best friend with all the qualities of loyalty, affection, and protection.

True symbols or archetypes have universal meanings. Water, blood, babies, and death are universal images which often appear in our dreams and aren't usually to be taken literally. For instance, if you dream of giving birth to a baby, it most likely doesn't mean that you're going to become pregnant. According to Cayce, babies represent new ventures or relationships; death symbolizes the letting go of a part of one's self; and water is the source of life. He identified snakes as meaning wisdom as well as kundalini energy. Animals and wild birds typically portray archetypal symbols of transcendence.

Jung believed archetypes can be likened to instinct. "Man's unconscious archetypal images are as instinctive as the ability of geese to migrate (in formation) . . . What we properly call instincts are physiological urges, and are perceived by the senses," he says. ". . . they also manifest themselves in fantasies and often reveal their presence only by symbolic images. . . what I call the archetypes. They are without known origin; and they reproduce themselves in any time or in any part of the world . . . " He also refers to them as "natural" symbols, which can be traced back to ideas and images of ancient and primitive societies.

Archetypal images are often used in Tarot cards and according to Osho, author of *Zen Tarot*, "They tell a journey of self-discovery that is absolutely unique to each individual, while the core truths to be discovered are the same regardless of race, gender, class, or religious upbringing."

Scriptures, myths, and fairy tales are filled with archetypal symbols. They are stories of humankind's origin and destiny, representing our struggle to find our way back to the Source. Shelley refers to the story of the prodigal son, the epic of the wanderings of Ulysses, the numerous tales of pilgrims, and of deposed princes struggling to regain their rightful kingdoms. "Each symbolic tale is variously embellished with other symbols which, though they seemingly refer to the outer world, are actually reflective of man's inner nature," she says. "Mountaintops—for instance—may well symbolize heightened consciousness. The rocky road up the mountain, the dangers and difficulties faced by the pilgrim, represent the obstacles in our own spiritual journey. Finding the similarities between the outer object and the inner meaning is the key to unlocking the message."

And these meanings are limited only by our imaginations. The more meaning we can evoke from a symbol, the more powerful it becomes. This is not a process of our intellect. Rather the meanings seep into our consciousness from the inner dialogues with our soul minds.

EXERCISE:

Spend the next few days looking for the symbolic power in your daily life. Do you see symbols being used in advertisements? Which types of symbols do advertisers use? Can you recognize the symbolic dimension of what you and others say, do, or wear? Notice the symbols of government, religion, or ethnic culture. Do certain images seem to present themselves to you unusually often? How do you respond to these symbols? Do you learn anything new about yourself or others by studying symbols?

PART ONE:
GUIDING LIGHTS—SIGNS, EMBLEMS, ARCHETYPES

Chapter 1

SYMBOLS: THE UNSPOKEN LANGUAGE OF THE UNIVERSE

The Cayce readings identify two ways of measuring your spiritual growth. One is through direct experience—to what degree you experience peace, joy, and purposefulness both within yourself and in your relationships with others. These fruits of the spirit, as they might be called, are the direct result of positive spiritual growth. They indicate that you have set a high spiritual ideal and are working in a disciplined way toward it. This isn't to say that life won't continue to have difficulties and challenges. But even these situations begin to feel more like opportunities. A challenge in life becomes an opportunity to apply spiritual insights and learn from the experience.

Cayce also says interpreting symbols is a way of measuring your spiritual growth. These symbols appear to you through communication with your own deeper consciousness. For example, every night when you dream, you are in contact with yourself that knows both your history and your potential as a spiritual being. This consciousness also engages you when you are awake, in meditation, or in moments of inspiration. But this deeper, wiser aspect of yourself speaks to you in the language of symbols which is quite different than the spoken or written word. If you are to benefit fully from the wisdom and insight which this level of your being can offer, you too need to learn this language. You need to grasp the reality in which this language is rooted, the reality of myth and dream. This spiritual reality is your true reality, which is your true home.

With these two sources of spiritual guidance—direct experience and symbolic language—you can develop an ongoing dialog with your soul. Unfortunately, the language of symbols isn't well known to most of us these days. Our ancestors, however, had a deep understanding of the use of symbols and myth and utilized them in their daily lives. They used symbols and rituals to address the mysteries of birth, death, and daily nourishment. Some of these symbols that have been found by archaeologists include Paleolithic cave paintings and small female figurines dating back to 30,000 B.C. These seem to be objects of worship symbolizing deities or spirits connected with the people's way of life.

Symbolic paintings, sculptures, even types of dress, all are expressions of symbolic meaning. The Egyptian ankh is a sign of eternal life and spiritual wisdom. The eye of Horus symbolizes the eye of God. The Native American symbol of the phoenix represents transformation, a death and rebirth, or a rising into a higher level of consciousness. All are highly complicated symbols from ancient cultures which can have meaning for us in today's modern technological world.

But even today, every culture on the earth, from primitive indigenous tribes to the most advanced members of the modern society, has its own very sophisticated set of symbols. These appear as flags, folk heroes, masks, and much more. Individually, you also have personal symbols. These are expressed in your dreams, in your actions, and even in the way you dress and the type of jewelry you wear. Cayce emphasized this in the following life reading to one woman:

> Yet those influences of being drawn by rote, by ritual, by peculiar dress, by peculiar habits, have their influence. (1183-1)

For many, however, very little weight is given to the language of symbol which has been replaced by the language of science. If something can be measured or weighed, then it exists. Otherwise it's said to be only a figment of the imagination.

Fortunately, in the last century, certain individuals have come forward to reaffirm an appreciation for the value of symbol and the myth. Carl Jung devoted his life to understanding both the nature and the language of the deeper mind, which he termed the unconscious. He described a symbol as the best possible expression of a truth that has not yet been grasped by the conscious mind. In his view the unconscious was continually trying to awaken or instruct the conscious mind to deeper levels of understanding. He called this awakening process "individuation." Joseph Campbell, one of the foremost authorities on world mythology, described a symbol as a kind of energy releaser. In some mysterious way certain images, stories, or actions put us in touch with reserves of energy which spring from the unconscious recesses of our human mind. Symbols, then, prompt us to greater achievements, both personally and culturally.

CAYCE'S CONTRIBUTION TO SYMBOLISM

The power of symbol is expressed richly in the Cayce readings. For example, in describing the condition of a person's soul, he used astrological symbolism. He also referred to past-life scenarios, some of which were set in prehistoric locations and periods such as Atlantis. In addition, hundreds of dreams were interpreted by Cayce. These dream readings effectively document how some symbols can be universal while others can be intensely personal. Edgar Cayce's own dreams and visions are a fascinating education into the world of symbols. On occasion while Cayce was giving a reading, another part of his mind was in the process of dreaming. Upon awakening he would often relate the dream to those around him.

On July 12, 1933, Cayce awoke from a reading and reported having had an experience which symbolically portrayed the process of giving a life reading. He saw himself traveling through water in a bubble and arriving at a place which he'd seen often in such visions: a great hall, which housed the books of life, one for every human being. Also there was an old man, the keeper of the books. Cayce walked up to the man and asked for the book of the person getting the reading. The old man handed him the book and as Cayce opened it the dream ended. A few months later during a question-and-answer reading, the entranced Cayce was asked to interpret the dream he'd experienced in July. The answer was an intriguing discourse on the nature and purpose of symbols:

> Q. What is the significance of the experience had during reading [373-2] Wednesday afternoon, July 12, in which Edgar Cayce saw himself traveling through water in a bubble and arriving at the place where he always gets the information—the old man with the books?
>
> A. To bring from one realm to another those experiences through which an entity, a soul, may pass in obtaining those reflections that are necessary for transmission of the information sought, it becomes

necessary (for the understanding of those in that realm seeking) to have that which is to the mental being put in the language of that being, as near as it is possible to do justice to the subject.

In this particular instance, then, to reach that record suggested by the suggestion itself—as of coming into existence across waters, the very thought of those present that it becomes necessary that that which is to receive or transmit the information must seek (as indicated by the manner in which periods, ages, dates, years, days are turned back, in arriving at the experience of the entity in a changed environ); meant that, the psychic influences in their activity with or through the physical forces of the body, must in some manner pass through the necessary elements for arriving at or reaching the beginning or that point. With the amount of water that is more often thought than of ether, what more befitting than that in the bubble the seeking forces should guide themselves!

Then, so becomes much that arrives in the material plane; in the form of pictures or expressions, that there may be the conveying to the mind of the seeker something in his own type of experience, as to how the transmission of the activity takes place. Of what forces? The psychic or soul forces, that are akin to what? The Creative Forces, or that called God.

So, the body in a symbolized form as the bubble arrives at a place in which there is kept the records of all; as signified in speaking of the Book of Life, or to indicate or symbolize that each entity, each soul in its growth, may find its way back to the Creative Influences that are promised in and through Him that gives—and is—life; and finds this as a separate, a definite, an integral part of the very soul.

Hence symbolized as being in books; and the man the keeper, as the keeper of the records. Much in the manner as would be said the lord of the storm, of the sea, of the lightning, of the light, of the day, of love, of hope, of faith, of charity, of long-suffering, of brotherly love, of kindness, of meekness, of humbleness, of self.

So, in the materialization for the concept of those that seek to know, to be enlightened: To the world, long has there been sought that as in books. To many the question naturally arises, then: Are there literally books? To a mind that thinks books, literally *books!* As it would be for the mind that in its passage from the material plane into rest would require Elysian fields with birds, with flowers; it must find the materialized form of that portion of the Maker in that realm wherein that entity, that soul, would enjoy such in *that* sphere of activity. As houses built in wood. Wood, in its essence, as given, is what? Books, in their essence, are what? What is the more real, the book with its printed pages, its gilt edges, or the essence of that told of in the book? (254-68)

The first paragraph of Cayce's answer says, in essence, that experiences in the spiritual realm need to be couched in images or metaphors that make sense to material consciousness. In other words, the images were symbolic.

The second paragraph interprets, in rather convoluted language, the symbolism of the water and the bubble. Then in paragraph three he summarizes beautifully the very purpose of symbols. "Then," he says, "so becomes much that arrives in the material plane; in the form of pictures or expressions, that there may be the conveying to the mind of the seeker something in his own type of experience, as to how the transmission of the activity takes place." In other words, symbols are images or pictures which we recognize but which suggest deeper meanings. Symbols put us in touch with the unseen mysteries of mind and spirit. Because of their depth of meaning they often carry an emotional impact. It's important to remember that symbols are more than just images, objects, or actions. They also include the feelings, insights, intuitions, and impressions which they stimulate inside you.

In paragraphs four and five of his answer, Cayce goes on to interpret the meaning of the books, which symbolize the soul's record, and the keeper of the books, which represents an aspect of the higher self. Then in paragraph six, Cayce presents us with an amazing proposition. He challenges us to consider the reality of the symbolic world. He says, "To many the question naturally arises, then, Are there literally books? To a mind that thinks books, literally *books!* As it would be for the mind that in its passage from the material plane into rest [meaning the passage of death] would require Elysian fields, with birds, with flowers . . . " Cayce is insisting that the symbolic realm is as real as the physical. Later in the paragraph he sets before us the essential question, posed rhetorically, so that his answer is clearly implied. "What is the more real?" he asks, " . . . the book with its printed pages, its gilt edges, or the essence of that told of in the book?" In other words, he implies that the ideas are at least as real, if not more so.

And there you have the central challenge in learning the language of your soul. Can you grasp the reality of symbols, even though they exist in a different dimension than that of time, space, and material objects? Carl Jung often stressed the point that dream symbols are spontaneous creations from the deeper mind. In other words, we don't make up symbols in our intellect and then apply meaning to them. Their meaning is beyond our immediate grasp. As we explore the meaning, we grow in consciousness. Our understanding expands. And that is exactly what a symbol is intended to do. Its very purpose is to make us grow. In fact we might as well go so far as to say that if we ever consciously understand everything that a symbol comes to reveal, then it ceases to operate as a true symbol. Symbols, even familiar ones, stretch us to understand more.

One woman gained an understanding of the symbolic meaning of her wedding and engagement rings after receiving an appraisal on them shortly after her divorce. Having a difficult marriage and one she knew she should have left many years before, she had no emotional attachment to the rings and only wished to be rid of them. She sat across from the appraiser's work area and handed him the rings. He took one look at her wedding ring and handed it back. "It's not worth appraising." She smiled, thinking only that it was because she had worn it thin from years of daily wear. He examined the engagement ring a little more closely and then sat back in the chair and sighed. "I can't charge you for the appraisal. It's only worth a retail replacement value of $125. You'd be lucky to get half of that." She thanked the man and left his office. On the way to the elevator she remembered that her husband paid $150. Her engagement ring was worth less now than it had been twenty years before. To her it symbolized that there was little value in her marriage.

DREAM SYMBOLS

Many dream symbols fall into one of two main categories: those that symbolize obstacles to your growth and those that symbolize new stages in your spiritual development. Your dream symbols can help you identify your destination and your detours. How do you know which is which? Well, the feelings associated with a symbol can sometimes be a clue. If a dream symbol generates a feeling of concern or alarm or similar emotion, it probably represents some feeling or attitude that is standing in the way of your spiritual growth.

The actual images of such symbols are often what you might expect. Therefore, shadowy figures, monsters, or threatening situations all may suggest some sort of barrier to your growth. Here's one example. In June 1933 Cayce dreamed that he and his wife, Gertrude, were in their car. He was driving the car through a narrow passage over muddy places where many other cars had gotten stuck. Yet he persevered and eventually came to some clear water and a nice road. Later that same day, Cayce asked in a reading for an explanation of that dream. The reading said, in part, that the dream reflected an anxiety of an upcoming trip, but at a deeper level the dream was symbolizing the struggles which the two of them were facing at that time in their lives. Those struggles were symbolized by the gorge, the rocks, and the narrow road. However, the dream also held a promise. It indicated that if the two of them held to their purpose they could make it through those difficult times and come to the clear water and the nice road, which symbolized new clarity of understanding and purity of purpose. This dream of Cayce's uses classic symbols for obstacles and barriers which can stand in our way. It also portrays the appropriate response to the barriers which the Cayces were facing. In the dream, Cayce cautiously threaded the car through the narrow way that was available to him and eventually, through careful persistence, he made it through.

Sometimes our subconscious speaks to us using symbols from our past experiences which may depict obstacles in more subtle or non-classic ways. These barriers are usually formed from experiences that made us feeling frustrated, limited, or caused us to have a sense of failure. For instance, Jack was fired from his job at a retail tire outlet early in his twenties, leaving him with a poor image of himself. Years later when he dreams of tires, he knows he's feeling less than adequate about himself within the context of a present-day situation.

On the other hand, dream symbols can also be direct glimpses of our potential. Some of the images that correspond to these symbols are brilliant light, an angel, a religious figure, or some significant role model. But they don't always have to be so grandiose. A young stockbroker in 1927 dreamed that he was smoking a particularly good cigar as he visited with his father. When he asked about this image in a reading, Cayce said that those symbols represented a new stage of harmony that was possible between the man and his father. The reading predicted that the new relationship would bring joy, satisfaction, contentment, even as there is seen in the smoking of the cigar.

OTHER SOURCES OF SYMBOLS

Not all symbols, of course, come from our dreams. We live in a virtual sea of symbols night and day. But we often don't recognize them as symbols. Flags in general are a fascinating example of symbolic language. They're also effective for explaining the distinction between true symbols and just signs, or insignias, because flags can be both.

Jung refers to flags as "cultural" symbols, which are often used in religions to express eternal truths. "They have gone through many transformations and even a long process of more or less conscious development, and have thus become collective images accepted by civilized societies," he says. "One is aware that they can evoke a deep emotional response in some individuals, and this psychic charge makes them function in much the same way as prejudices."

The stars and stripes symbolizes the United States. The flag of the hammer and sickle used to represent the Soviet Union. The union jack brings about thoughts of Britain. However, if these emblems take on wider circles of meaning for a person, they can become symbolic. The meanings of the symbols are like ripples in a pond. They're constantly expanding outward. For many people the flag of the stars and stripes means much more than just a label. It may symbolize home and family, freedom and fair play, Mom and apple pie. To a patriotic Russian the hammer and sickle may have represented social comradeship, equality, and the motherland all at the same time. It's our association with emblems that make them symbolic. To one person a cigar may mean an obnoxious annoyance. To the dreamer mentioned earlier it meant joy, satisfaction, and contentment. By itself a cigar is just a cigar. It becomes symbolic when it's associated with other thoughts and experiences that expand into the unconscious. This is suggested in the following reading for a sixty-five-year-old man, a psychologist and brain specialist:

> In the emblematical—the entity is ever the torch-bearer; and this should be as an emblem to remind the self of the needs of purity and of life, that the truth itself may be the more readily grasped by those who seek . . . (1851-1)

For instance, we're taught that a red octagon on a post at an intersection means stop. But a stop sign only means stop because we associate the shape and the word with that command. Again, it's our peculiar power to attribute meanings to images that creates a stop sign, or any sign—or language itself, for that matter. For language is nothing more than an attachment of meaning to sounds and visual designs.

However, symbols differ from signs in one important way. There is no mystery to a sign. A stop sign means stop and that's the end of it. A stop sign doesn't draw you toward a deeper understanding of something. A symbol, on the other hand, always means more than you can put your finger on. Its field of meaning is constantly expanding. The more you ponder a symbol, the more it means to you. As you contemplate a symbol, it generates a growth of consciousness.

According to Joseph Campbell, a symbol performs two simultaneous functions. On one hand it opens a person to the inexpressible spiritual realities which are beyond words, while at the same time it anchors a person to the specific context of the symbol's unique form. Religious symbols are of this kind. The star of David, the cross, the star and crescent—all can lead people to an awareness of the universal, nameless spiritual reality. Yet their symbolic power is most effective when people embrace a specific one with total devotion. Take, for example, the symbol of the cross. At a certain level the cross is just an insignia of a particular religion. But at the same time it can be symbolic of all of the mystery and passion of the universal spiritual experience. Over the years the cross has carried extraordinary symbolic power, but mostly for those who embraced it with singular devotion. In the Middle Ages, all of Europe banded together under the cross and marched into the Holy Land to liberate Jerusalem from the infidels. The war was even named The War of the Cross, or The Crusades. A cross was sewn onto the tunic of each soldier who called himself a crusader.

This Cayce reading states just one example of the meaning of the cross:

Q. What is the meaning of the cross?
A. The Christ. (294-204)

During one episode of this lengthy war, the crusaders were engaged in a losing battle. They were exhausted, starved, and completely demoralized. They faced overwhelming odds and almost certain death. Yet one soldier, rummaging around in the basement of an ancient church, found a piece of wood which he identified as a piece of the true cross—in other words, part of the actual cross on which Jesus had been crucified. Bolstered by the find of this most sacred relic, the crusaders rallied and won the day. Now such a story can only be understood by recognizing the tremendous symbolic force which the cross held for those crusaders. It makes no difference whether that piece of wood was actually from the original cross. What matters is that they believed it to be so. That belief elevated them to such a spiritual ecstasy that they acquired almost miraculous strength.

Religious symbols can have phenomenal power, which can be channeled either creatively or destructively. The crusaders also used the symbol of the cross to justify the massacres of innocent non-Christians. The best way to keep symbols working positively is to recognize them as symbols. Look through the symbol and identify to some extent what it represents to you. Of course, no symbol can be fully explained. If it can, it's not really a symbol. But you can think of a symbol as a stained glass window. It shapes and colors the light of ideals. Yet it's the light and not the pattern that is the greatest value. There are many other symbols that populate our world. While few of them reach the depths of religious symbols, they do carry mental, emotional, and spiritual associations.

In a certain sense, any aspect of life can be symbolic if the unconscious mind makes it so. Things and events become symbolic when deeper and wider meanings apply to them. For example, what is a new car? Is it a piece of machinery used to transport people and goods from place to place? Or is it a symbol of success, self-esteem, and sex appeal?

For one woman, a new car symbolized freedom. She was in a troubled marriage and had a car that was quite dangerous to drive due to a leaky fuel pump, which posed a potential fire hazard. She often found herself stranded along the roadside and forced to rely on friends and family members to help her because her husband was unreachable or unwilling to help. When she proposed buying a new car, he objected and told her to make do with what she had. Without his consent, she purchased a new car on her own and within a few weeks left her marriage. While her old car symbolized the unreliability of her relationship with her husband, the new car symbolized freedom and the start of a whole new life, one that held the virtues of reliability and dependability.

Another woman cleaned out her closet and bought new clothes after her children left home and she started a new career. Clothing, hair styles, jewelry—all possess a symbolic potential, as do names. Here Cayce explains the importance of names to the Glad Helpers Healing Prayer Group:

> There is a Name to each soul. For He hath called His own *by name!* . . .Was one named John by chance? Was one named Joe or Llewellyn by chance? No; they are relative! . . . but these carry then the vibrations of same; and in the end the name is the sum total of what the soul-entity in all of its vibratory forces has borne toward the Creative Force itself! (281-30)

We use name changes, new hair styles, and even new styles of clothing to symbolize important changes in our lives. We incorporate them into rituals, which are themselves symbolic actions. For example, after the death of his wife, one man took their two wedding rings to a jeweler and melted them together into a single ring. In this way the new ring symbolized for him the unity they shared which continued beyond the vale of death. However, another man, jilted by his fiancé, traded in her returned engagement ring for a man's ring which fit nicely onto his third finger. Both of these men ritualized their feelings into symbolic acts which helped them through a difficult life transition. One divorced woman burned her wedding dress in a small private ceremony in the woods. This act symbolized her new life rising up from the ashes of her "old" married life.

CONSCIOUSLY ENGAGING SYMBOLS

The Cayce readings demonstrated a deep understanding of the practical use of symbols. They often recommended symbols of one kind or another to help an individual toward greater spiritual development. Occasionally Cayce advised an individual to change his or her name, a new name symbolizing a new state of consciousness:

> The body would do well to change its name . . . from Carl to Michael [. . .] and then start over again and do more lecturing and living up to that. (5023-2)

Sometimes the readings advised individuals to wear stones of different color and composition. Some of these readings alluded to a physical vibration of the stone, but most often Cayce said it was the meaning of the stone's color and formation to the person. In other words, the stone carried symbolic power. Here are two examples, the first for a young man, age nineteen, and the second for a female, age forty-five:

> As to the material inclinations—we find things that become what might be termed as omens. Not that these should be merely considered as good luck stones that the entity should wear about self often, or most always—but the lapis liqurius [?] would bring much that will act in that manner as would be termed a *protective* influence, if kept about the entity. (1931-1)

> Hence we find these as those things that should be in the form of omens about the body; not as good luck charms, but they may be termed so by many; for these are from those activities and sojourns that will make for variations in the *vibrations* about the entity, hence bringing much more of harmony into the experience of the entity in the present activity: The very red stones; as of coral, that is rather of the deep sea variety, and when this is worn about the neck or about the waist—or upon the arm—let it rest upon the flesh, for it will bring quiet to the body. (694-2)

Other people were advised to carry or wear certain religious symbols, sometimes Christian, sometimes Jewish, sometimes ancient Egyptian. People were told that such symbols would help awaken their spiritual awareness. Which symbol depended on the meaning it conveyed to the individual soul. The following reading was given to a fifty-four-year-old housewife:

> A Maltese cross of teakwood should be worn by

the entity at all times, next to the skin, about the neck or waist. It will be seen from experiences in the material plane, as well as the symbols from same, that this would have a helpful influence by creating a *vibration*. Not that it would within itself have an influence, but the associations of same would become as helpful influences—just as that you think gradually grows to become *you*—as you digest its influence or force. (2029-1)

Symbols affect our consciousness whether we are aware of them or not. So it's wise to become aware of the symbols that surround our daily lives and visit us in our dreams. In the following chapter, you will learn about dream symbology. But before moving on, take a few moments to reflect upon some of your personal symbols.

EXERCISE:

Think about:

Your wardrobe—what does it say about you as a person?

Your hair style—have you changed it at any significant junctures in your life?

Your jewelry—is there any particular piece of jewelry that has some significance for you?

Chapter 2

DREAM SYMBOLS

Dreams, visions, impressions, to the entity in the normal sleeping state are the presentations of the experiences necessary for the development, if the entity would apply them in the physical life. These may be taken as warnings, as advice, as conditions to be met, conditions to be viewed in a way and manner as lessons, as truths, as they are presented in the various ways and manners. (294-70)

Each night you spend approximately ninety minutes in a dream state. Some of us can remember all or most of our dreams, and others have trouble remembering even a snippet from one of our nightly sojourns.

The dream state is an experimental playground which gives you a chance to explore and express emotions without the usual inhibitions you may display in your waking life. Dreams provide an avenue of expression for that part of yourself that knows both your history and your potential as a spiritual being. They are another way the universe provides guidance about relationships, careers, and health problems. Through dreams you may find answers to your spiritual questions and even receive encouragement to some challenge in your life. While some dreams may allow you to release bottled emotions from your day's activities, others can be profoundly insightful in a psychological or spiritual way.

However, Jung said dreams are "the main source of all of our knowledge about symbolism." This means that the messages you receive from your dreams are expressed symbolically and must be interpreted to find their true meaning.

Mark Thurston, executive director for A.R.E. and author of *Dreams: Tonight's Answers for Tomorrow's Questions*, says, "A dream symbol is the very *best* way for your unconscious self to communicate to your conscious self. The particular image chosen—be it an object, a person, an animal, or whatever—has shades of meaning and personal associations that make it the best communicator of some truth about yourself."

The Chinese believe that it is your spiritual soul which creates your dreams and leaves the body to travel to other realms and meet other souls. They and other ancient cultures, including the Greeks, erected dream temples for seekers to find guidance about their lives. Many times purification rituals as well as other rites of preparation were performed by the seeker prior to entering the temple and the dream state. Upon awakening, the seeker consulted with the temple dream interpreters.

According to James R. Lewis, in *The Dream Encyclopedia*, "Up to the sixteenth century, government officials were required to visit dream temples to receive guidance and insight before instituting any political policies or official declarations." While this may not have been standard practice in all parts of the world, it is interesting to note that in some areas heads of government put credence in their dreams. But you don't have to be a government leader to experience help from your dreams in making decisions. As Cayce put it:

Harken to thy dreams and visions, for these may
oft be channels through which ye may be known,
be made known to impending disturbances, or the
choice to be made for the better universality in the
activities. (5264-1)

Cayce believed that our dreams served several functions. Somatic dreams—dreams referring to the body—
are extremely important to be mindful of. Very often
dreams will offer solutions to health problems. Steve was
plagued with food allergies for many years, but was un-
able to find the source of his discomfort. Then one night
he went to bed and he saw a can of coffee. He quit drinking coffee and his symptoms disappeared.

Some dreams point to the emotional cause of the
physical problem. Celia, a college student, had been
plagued a year and a half with bladder infections. They
seemed to appear almost instantaneously after conflicts
involving her father, with whom she had had a strained
relationship for many years and which became even
more tense with the separation and divorce of her parents. One night Celia's mom, who had been extremely
concerned and sorrowful about the rift between her
daughter and her ex-husband, had a dream that Celia's
bladder problems were going to kill her. A woman doctor appeared in the dream and said it was going to end
her life. This woman was an acquaintance of Celia's mom
and was suffering from cancer. Celia's mom woke up
from the dream distressed and worried that her daughter was dying. But after reflecting upon the dream and
sharing it with several friends, she realized that her
daughter was being "eaten up" by the anger and frustra-
tion she felt because of her father's lack of love for her.
Yet it was a warning that it could end her life, perhaps
emotionally, if something wasn't done to correct the situation.

Jung says that rarely do the symbols in your dreams have just one meaning. And when interpreting the messages in your dreams, he suggests going with your first hunch, relying on your intuitive abilities, before applying more rational methods of dream interpretation.

Clear vivid recall is also a signal. One woman reports that she always pays attention to the early morning dreams, for she knows these are special messages from God. They can appear as images, as spoken word, or even typed messages. Other individuals report having significant dreams occur just after falling asleep. It's important to learn how your own individual rhythms and your dream psychology work.

RECURRENT DREAMS

These are by and large dreams that are really key issues in the person's life at that time. The dream's not going to go away until you deal with the issue which is presented. Even figuring out what the dream is referring to is not necessarily going to make the dream go away. At workshops and conferences, Thurston frequently tells about a dream that he had in college where he showed up for English class only to find they were having a test, and he wasn't prepared because he skipped several recent sessions. This dream recurs when he's not doing what he needs to be doing to be prepared.

Dreams can also be a way of working with our shadow side. Violent dreams may be a warning that we may be watching too many violent movies. Or they could be an indication that something we're eating is having a negative effect on our physical bodies and our process of elimination. "Assuming that a person's not overdoing it on violent movies, there is still probably within us all a certain measure of a shadow that has a violent quality to it that's integrated into our whole personality," says

Thurston. "When we have a dream in which we're be-
having violently, it may be just an invitation to get in
touch with that side of ourselves rather than block it off
and exile it by denying it."

Thurston says dreams tend to give us a more honest
picture of who we are. "We are such diverse creatures,
sometimes the word 'real self' is used as a synonym for
higher self or best self. It seems to me in our dreams we
get both extremes," he explains. "We get glimpses of a
deeper, more centered, clearer side of ourselves from
time to time. But I think we also get dreams of our so-
called shadow side of ourselves, which is a kind of darker,
less socialized, rawer side of ourselves. It's in a sense
looking with greater honesty at all the parts of who we
are. That's why it's important to take a look at your
dreams over a longer span of time."

He suggests asking yourself how can you work creatively with that kind of raw, violent energy and perhaps
using that vitality for some good cause. "If there's something in us that's angry and capable of getting angry, that
same energy can be used purposely to make changes in
the world, to make changes in ourselves," says Thurston.

If you're having dreams in which you're frequently getting mad at someone, it's not necessarily guidance to
start blowing your stack at that person. It may just be an
indication that there needs to be some changes in the
relationship. There may be an issue that needs to be dis-
cussed before it destroys the relationship. On the other
hand, if you're in a relationship in which healthy communication is not possible, the dream may indicate that
there is a lot of energy invested in the relationship. You
may have to discover purposeful and constructive ways
to work with that raw energy without engaging the other
person in an actual physical discussion. Repressing the
anger or the energy is not going to be healthy for the self
or for the relationship.

THE ROLES OF OTHERS IN YOUR DREAMS

Dreaming about other people may be a way of seeing another side of yourself. What are the characteristics of that person that may remind you of something inside of yourself? If you dream of an authoritarian figure, such as a police officer, question whether you are in some way being overbearing in some situation.

It's important to be open to explore not only your relationship with that person but also what he or she signifies to you. Look at all the options.

For instance, if you dream of a man in the next neighborhood who drives a new Lexus, you may not be literally dreaming about him or any part of yourself which he represents. But perhaps his new, expensive car makes you feel inadequate because you're driving around town in a ten-year-old car with dents and rusted fenders.

Edgar Cayce also believed that deceased friends and family members do occasionally visit us in our dream state. These occurrences may offer direct communication with those people or allow us to resolve our feelings about their death. The person may also represent some aspect of ourselves.

If you have a dream in which you are physically intimate with someone, it could be suggestive of an innate or natural kind of affinity which the two of you have, usually on a psychological, emotional, or spiritual level. It isn't necessarily guidance from God or one's higher self to start an affair.

SYMBOLIC DREAMS

One night Karen dreamt that she was driving to a castle, scraping the side of the car as she entered the gate. Inside the castle there were two men, who appeared friendly upon meeting her. But once they got her inside, they stripped her of her clothes, except for the shirt on her back. They left the room, but she was aware that they intended to rape her when they returned. All around the castle was an electrical fence or force field which prevented her from leaving. Then a telephone rang, she answered it, and a friend asked if she needed help. Karen said she did but she didn't know where she was, but to send the police, and she'd scream when they got near. Karen was extremely shaken by this dream. With the help of the members of her study group, she was able to determine that the men represented her estranged husband, who appeared friendly upon meeting, but over the course of their marriage "raped" her of her dignity and her financial stability, leaving her with a mound of debt and little more than the shirt on her back. In recent weeks she'd been having contact with him, but became extremely upset each time she did. The electrical fence symbolized the emotional charge which was keeping her under the influence of his power. The dream also indicated that she could call for help, and it would appear.

ARCHETYPAL IMAGES

Frequently universal symbols appear in dreams. Carl Jung says that the archetypes or symbols reflected in the world's mythology and folklore form our collective unconscious. This is the storehouse of all of humanity's experiences which also emerge in our dream images. He referred to dreams containing these images as "grand dreams." For instance the inner child, our playful creative self that is usually sacrificed upon entering adulthood, usually appears in our dreams as a fully clothed and functioning child. The divine child archetype is a symbol of our total self, according to Jung, and is often symbolized as a powerful image in our dreams.

Circles are also archetypal images, representing the self, which can appear in dreams. Jung referred to these as mandalas. These frequently appear during stressful times and indicate a need for harmony and balance.

Joseph Campbell had his own views on mythological images which occur in our dreams. "[D]ream is a personal experience of that deep, dark ground that is the society's dream. The myth is the public dream and the dream is the private myth," he said in his interview with Bill Moyers on *The Power of Myth*. "If your private myth, your dream, happens to coincide with that of society, you are in good accord with your group. If it isn't, you've got an adventure in the dark forest ahead of you."

That dark forest may appear as death. Death is also a metaphorical universal symbol which could indicate a death of a relationship, or of a self-image, or a need to let go of some situation. Cayce was frequently called upon to interpret dreams where individuals dreamed of death, either of their own or of someone else's. On many occasions he stated that the death portrayed in the dream was referring to a death of some part of the individual, be it a state of mind or an attitude.

Perhaps it's most important to remember that these symbolic images, according to Thurston, are closely related to the experiences we have in our conscious waking lives. Cayce called our daily life experiences which impact the dream "the physical or mental experiences of the body," as stated in the following reading:

Dreams or visions are the subconscious forces of an entity while the conscious forces are subjugated, and the experience for the mind of the soul (or the subconscious) is often tempered by the physical or mental experiences of the body, and when such is the case these then are presented often in emblematical ways and manners. (302-3)

TELEPATHIC DREAMS

The mind has an extraordinary ability to tune in to the thoughts and feelings of someone else. This most frequently occurs in a relationship where there is caring— what Cayce called "the love intent." This could be with a spouse, a friend, your parents, or your children. Because you've invested energy and positive intentions with your waking, conscious mind, it makes sense that your unconscious would explore the deeper levels of connection with that person, too.

One woman received a telepathic dream from a man in her life, telling her that he wanted to be with her. This dream appeared the night after she visited him in his hospital room after he had minor surgery, only to find another woman there who obviously had designs on him. She was naturally upset over the accidental meeting, especially since he had voiced intentions of their spending time together and also of their special connection with each other. She left the hospital, went home, and fell asleep crying. In the middle of the night, she had a dream that the telephone was ringing, and he was on the other end. He said, "You're the one I want to be with." She accepted this message as an indication that they would eventually be together, coupled with other intuitive messages she had felt over the course of their developing relationship.

CONTACT WITH GOD

Through dreams the entity may gain the more perfect understanding of the relationships between God and [humanity], and the way in which . . . God, manifests through mankind. (900-143)

One man reports that occasionally he hears a voice in

his dreams. This voice usually is loud and strong and is not associated with any characters in his dreams. "Typically, I'm told something very specific to do or not to do," he relates. "I know this is God speaking to me—loud and clear. And I know I'd better listen."

Morton Blumenthal, who received more dream interpretations from Cayce than anyone else—in fact, more readings than anyone else—often reported dreams of a disembodied "voice," which offered counsel. Cayce usually indicated this was input from the Creative Forces. For example, in one dream, Blumenthal dreamt of a figure leading him by the hand, and a voice which said, "The Lord will lead you—but you must . . . " He had forgotten the rest of what was said to him, but Cayce interpreted it as follows:

> As in this, as is seen, again and again, the entity receives that reassurance of the higher forces guiding, guarding, and directing the entity in its actions, as it were, with the cloud by day and the pillar of fire by night. (900-266)

Morton also had a fascinating dream in which God came to visit him. To the dreamer's surprise, God was a modern businessman. Cayce's interpretation pointed out that God was someone with whom we can "do business." God is not only transcendent but also actively involved in human affairs. It was a powerful message and, in a sense, a wonderful revelation from the Divine.

PROPHETIC DREAMS

At times our dreams can provide us with a glimpse of the future. During a particularly stressful period in my life where a situation I was involved with had become quite difficult, I had a dream of standing knee deep in

the Chesapeake Bay, near where I live. Dolphins were cir-
cling just in front of me. Navy ships were moving off to
the right going away from me. I interpreted this dream
to mean that the "war," represented by the ships, would
soon be over. The dolphins symbolized peace and harmony for me. A week later, I did, indeed, feel peace about
the situation, and I was reminded of the dream as I was
taking my morning walk along the bay. I had let my dog
loose for a swim and was standing in the water up to my
knees. A few yards away dolphins were swimming in
circles and in the distance navy ships were moving out
to sea.

COMPENSATORY DREAMS

Occasionally our subconscious will show us ways to
balance our waking life through situations in our dreams.
For instance, if we dream of a raging fire, yet deny that
we have any anger toward a situation or person, perhaps
it's a clue to tune in to our true feelings and allow our
anger to vent in healthy ways. If we dream of being in a
bookstore but we're not very interested in books, it may
be a call to read.

Compensatory dreams are really just a call to find balance or moderation in our lives.

PAST-LIFE DREAMS

Memories from our past lives may also appear in our
dreams, often to help us with current situations. "These
past-life influences can sometimes be as subtle as using
chopsticks to convey an Oriental incarnation, or they
can be much more vivid and obvious with period cos-
tumes, locations, etc.," says Nancy Pohle, public information officer for A.R.E. and also co-author of the soon
to be published A.R.E. Press book, *Awakening the Real*

You. "The important point to remember though is not who or where we were at a given time, but how that lifetime impacts and influences us now."

For example, shortly after meeting David, Rebecca had a dream about being in medieval times. In it she saw a man on a horse riding toward her and felt a warm glow in her heart. When she woke up, she realized that David was the man in her dream, which explained the incredible amount of love she felt for David, even though they had met only a few weeks before.

Also note that what may appear as a "past life" in a dream or a vision may really be symbolizing some aspect of a current situation metaphorically. Instead of getting hooked onto the past-life drama, look at the action in the dream or vision for clues to a present-life situation.

INTERPRETING YOUR DREAMS

The methods mentioned in this section are only meant to prime the pump so to speak and inspire you to delve deeper into the methods of dream interpretation. There are numerous books in print which can provide in-depth instruction on dream interpretation. You may want to start with the following: *Dreams—Your Magic Mirror* by Elsie Sechrist; *Dreams: Tonight's Answers for Tomorrow's Questions* by Mark Thurston, Ph.D.; *Edgar Cayce on Dreams* by Harmon Bro; as well as *The Edgar Cayce Readings: Dreams and Dreaming, Parts I and II.*

Cayce said it is important to have a "correct" purpose for working with our dreams. A desire to improve our lives is also crucial. He says this of dreams:

... [they] are phenomena, or experiences for a body to use, to apply, in its everyday walk of life . . . the body must approach [the interpretation] with

> the correct purpose . . . While this may be explained
> . . . for the . . . entity, the whole reaction must be
> *solely* within self . . . these are [given so] that one
> may have an understanding of how to apply in self
> that that self already has in hand, to the betterment
> of self . . . (4167-1)

"Once this 'correct purpose' is part of our consciousness, we can begin to work productively with our
dreams," says Pohle. "It's also essential to write down
your spiritual, mental, and physical ideals before working with your dreams. These serve as the standard by
which you can measure your progress, and they help focus attention on what is truly important."

Each night while you're sleeping, your soul mind is
sending you messages, and these messages might very
well have the answers for some important decisions
you're about to make, contact from deceased relatives,
clues about an illness you may be suffering, or just gentle
reminders to give an old friend a call. But you'll never
understand these messages if you don't take the time to
write your dreams down and make an attempt to interpret their meanings.

"It's often with hindsight that you recognize the messages in your dreams. If you're not writing them down,
then you'll lose about ninety percent of the possibilities of what your dreams are trying to tell you," says
Thurston. "It is not only important to reflect upon your
dreams in a daily fashion, but also to look over the
dreams you've had for the past month, six months, or a
year.

"Each of us has different ways to relax, and prefer different kinds of foods and vacation, and so we have different idiosyncrasies in the way our dreams unfold," he
adds.

It's important to keep a dream journal and a pen or

pencil near your bed. It needn't be fancy, even a loose leaf notebook will do. And if you have a partner, a small flashlight would be helpful to keep handy as well, that way he or she won't be disturbed when you wake at 3:00 in the morning to jot down your dreams.

Write down everything you can remember. Sometimes just a few words are all that some people need in order to jog their memories in the morning. Others need to write down every sequence that they can remember. Keeping an index of the symbols that appear in your dream is also helpful. This way you develop personal meanings of those symbols that appear in your dreams.

If you have trouble remembering your dreams, there are several helpful methods to try, including sleep suggestions and keeping paper and pencil by your bedside. Another technique to try is drinking a large glass of water before going to bed. Your body will surely rouse you in the middle of the night. But before leaping up to dash off to the bathroom, lie still and search your consciousness for any hints of a dream. After two or three nights with the water drinking, you'll probably have trained your mind to awaken during the night right after dreaming, and then you can skip the water at bedtime.

No matter what recall-enhancing method you choose, it may take some practice before you begin remembering the details of your dreams. In some cases you may get only a sensation or feeling upon awakening. Write it down and ponder it in the morning. Images may appear as you reflect upon the feeling.

When you are successful at remembering a significant portion of a dream—symbols, story line, feelings, and all—take some time to reflect upon the meaning your dreams may hold for you. Ask yourself questions like these to help gain insight about the dream's meaning:

• How am I different for having gone through that dream experience?

- How has the dream changed my attitudes about a person or a situation?
- If this had been a waking-life experience, what would I have learned from it?
- What way might this dream bring balance into my life? That is to say, is there an extreme in this dream and could it have come to balance the opposite of that extreme in my waking life?

There are several clues that indicate a dream may have a special message for you. If your dream is very vivid or elicits a strong emotional response, these are flags that the dream is worthy of extra attention.

Dreams are real. Even if you don't remember them, you are being affected and changed. The more puzzling they are, the more important it is to unravel the messages they hold.

Pohle says, "In whatever manner our dream messages come to us, we should always look at how they can enhance our purpose for being in the earth and strengthen our relationship with the Creative Forces and with one another."

Dreams are experiences of the soul. If we remember them, we can put these insights to better use. By doing so we bring our life into harmony with our highest good and greatest potential. If we consciously remember our dreams and work with them, we can use them as a tool for growth and self-study. Cayce emphasized this in the following reading:

> Correlate those truths that are enacted in each and every dream . . . and use such to the better developing, ever remembering develop means going toward the higher forces, or the Creator. (3744-4)

Shortly after Anna moved to a new city and began a new job, she had a dream about being a plane. She actu-

ally had the feeling that her arms were her wings. She
was flying a mission above the ocean and below her were
large navy ships. She also had a sense that other planes
were with her. She was flying along, but a great fear of
being shot down prevented her from flying smoothly.
She (the plane) dipped and wobbled, and she was very
aware of the ships with their big guns. But then she had a
shift in consciousness, and she concentrated only on flying. She discovered that she really was having fun flying
and even turned over and flew with the belly of the plane
(the front of her body) toward the sky, her back to the
ships. Above her was the vast expanse of the night sky
and beautiful glimmering stars. Anna awoke with a wonderful sense of peace and interpreted this as a sign that
she needed to let go of her worries.

From the feeling she had when she awoke, Anna realized that the plane symbolized herself, an interpretation
she arrived at from the sensations that her body became
the plane. The sky represented the presence of the Divine in her life, and the awe she experiences when she
allows herself to feel the guidance and protection of her
Creator. The ships, which were threatening to shoot her
down, were people from her "old" life who didn't agree
with her belief system or the choices she had recently
made, and in fact had verbally wished ill upon her. The
other planes flying along with her were her supportive
friends, lots of them.

After jotting the dream down in her journal, Anna reflected on the portion of the dream where she feared
being shot down. Rationally, it made no sense. Life was
going very well for her, better than it ever had. She was
making a number of new friends, she was having success in her new job, and spiritual, gentle men were entering her life. But deep inside was an anxiety that it
would all be swept away. Her dream was clearly a message from the universe to stop worrying and just go

about her "flying"—her daily activities—and enjoy all the wonderful experiences of her life. She was being told to soar. She shared the dream in her study group, and many agreed that she made the correct interpretation.

UNDERSTANDING YOUR PERSONAL SYMBOLS

To gain a better understanding of your dreams, you need to recognize the symbols that influence your life *and* to develop an understanding of the meaning behind these symbols, some of which may be readily apparent. For instance, Nancy knew that when she was having car problems, it was a signal for her to slow down. And when she noticed the gas gauge nearing empty, it was time for her to "refuel" herself.

At other times, however, the meanings of our symbols can be puzzling, and we may need to work with them to uncover their relevance to our spiritual journey. Here's how Cayce did that interpretative work for one person:

A circle, a tree—as the tree of life, whose very leaves are not as of the poplar, not as the willow, not as the lichen, but rather the fruit; not only the fruit which sustains life as the words and acts of the entity, but that which give within same the very life or fruit thereof itself—with the cross. Not the cross upon the tree nor the tree as a cross. Rather the cross as the bridge between understanding and ignorance, as may be upon either side of same, with those words upon the ribbon—*Cum Et Laudus*—or—*Laudi—Understanding is the greatness in wisdom in thy fellow man.* (246-02)

The following exercise may help you in your clarification process. It's called *symbol amplification*, and it was developed by Dr. Carl Jung. It's a kind of free association, i.e., letting things pop into your mind spontaneously— but it differs from Freudian free association. Freud preferred to take a symbol and let the client free associate from one image to the next, drifting further and further away. Here the questions, some of which may not be relevant to the symbol, focus on the symbol:

Symbol Amplification:

1. What is a(n) _____?

2. What does a(n) _____ do?

3. What does a(n) _____remind me of?

4. What do I like about a(n) _____?

5. What do I dislike about a(n) _____?

6. What kind of person would use (or be involved with) a(n) _____?

7. What benefits does a(n) ____provide?

8. What problems does a(n) ____create?

9. What advantages (or disadvantages) are there in having a(n) ____?

You can also carry on a dialogue with your symbols, whether it's a person, an animal, a location, or an inanimate object. For instance if you dream of a dolphin, here are some important questions you can ask:

1. Do you have a name?

2. Where have you just come from?

3. What were you doing there?

4. What do you like best about being (a dolphin)?

5. What don't you like about being (a dolphin)?

6. What do you most desire?

7. What do you most fear?

8. How do you feel about (one of your other symbols)?

9. What do you have in common with these other symbols?

10. What would you like to say to me right now?

Please keep in mind that these questions may only be a way to warm up the interaction between you and your symbol. You may think of more questions to ask. Feel free to keep going and write down the answers you receive. Gayle Delaney's book, *Living Your Dreams*, is a good resource for further instruction on clarifying the meanings of symbols in your dreams.

You may also elicit some clarification by doing a little research into your symbols. Consult a dictionary, encyclopedia, or any other source that may be helpful to you in defining the meanings.

Thurston reminds us: "Almost every dream symbol— especially the two types we have called emblems and universal symbols—are rich in subtle meanings," he writes in *Dreams: Tonight's Answers for Tomorrow's Questions*. "No single word or phrase accurately captures all of what it conveys and reveals to you. Not only does the symbol contain within it a message your intellectual mind can grasp; it also works on you at a nonverbal, emotional level."

EXERCISE:

Begin your personal dream journal. Reserve a few pages in the front or the back for an index of symbols that appear frequently in your dreams. Leave it near your bed with a pen or pencil and a small flashlight. Begin recording your dreams each and every morning.

Share your dreams with a friend and do a little brainstorming on the meanings some of the symbols may have for you. Remember there is no single answer. The one that feels right to you is the right one.

Chapter 3

Symbolism in Life Seals

Let the seal as indicated be as an emblem—not in the form of something to be worn, but something to be studied each morning or evening when ye would analyze thyself and the motives of others. (1770-3)

One of the most intriguing tools found in the Cayce readings is the personalized life seal. Cayce believed that life seals could be used to stimulate or quicken spiritual development. The life seal is essentially a picture comprised of symbols which carry deeply significant meaning to a person's soul. To use the life seal, the readings suggested having it artistically drawn according to its description, although at times Cayce suggested that the individual draw his or her own life seal, as in the following reading:

As to emblems and figures, these have meant and do at times mean a great deal, or they bring a message to the entity in the varied forms and manners.

The seal of life (and it will be well for the entity itself to draw this, for the very act will come a concept of the union of Creative Energy or God and self, or the ego that makes application of these meanings). (1825-1)

Cayce also suggested that the owner of the seal put it in a prominent place where he or she could see it often during the day. The visual impression of the symbols was said to stimulate the spiritual consciousness of its owner. In other words, the life seal symbolized the person's highest spiritual development. By viewing it, an individual was inspired toward his or her own destiny.

"Symbols can serve as reminders, to our conscious minds and to our unconscious minds, of who we are and why we are here," says Shelley in *Symbols and the Self.*

Here is an example of how Cayce described a life seal in reading 308-9:

The seal here as would be indicated would be the leaf; not the palm and yet not the Canadian leaf, yet not the corn, but a long leaf with the erosions on the side much as the oak leaf. This would be green and red in color. The signs or seals about same would be: above the leaf and very small, a helmet; not that of the latter day but more in the form of the knighted helmet. This would be with the cross and the staff crossed behind same. This would indicate the might, the universality, and the strength in the cross and the staff.

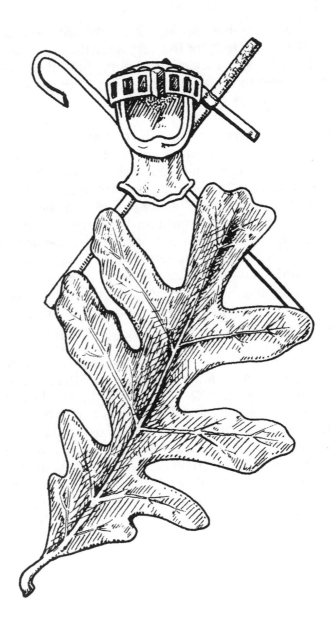

While many readings volunteered life seal descriptions, this individual asked for one. It's fascinating how this reading took great pains to describe a very specific shape of leaf. At the end of the first line it begins . . . *not the palm and yet not the Canadian leaf, yet not the corn, but a long leaf with the erosions on the side much as the oak leaf.* And you'll see that the artist did a pretty good job of following that rather involved description. The other symbols, then, are quite straightforward: the knighted helmet, the cross, and the staff. The reading then offered some interpretation to these symbols. It says at the end, *This would indicate the might, the universality, and the strength in the cross and in the staff.*

Cayce also gave aura chart readings in addition to the life seals readings, both of which confirmed the continuity of life. Both were usually preceded by life readings which, according to Shelley in her book, described individuals' past lives in the earth and affirmed the eternal qualities of the soul.

"The aura chart readings gave instruction for the drawing of pictures and symbols which would suggest various past lives. They were meant to appeal to the subconscious minds of the people for whom they were given, and to aid in their development," she writes. "The life seals, although not as detailed and complex as the aura charts, were also descriptions of individuals' symbols and were meant to lift the aspirations of the conscious mind as well as to impress subliminally the subconscious mind."

The whole purpose for the life seal, and all of symbology for that matter, is neatly expressed in a few words. It produces a trend of mind that is excellent for spiritual unfolding. Now, wouldn't you like to have a life seal of your own to help stimulate your spiritual unfolding? But how can you get one without a Cayce reading to obtain the symbols and descriptions? The readings themselves insist that we can do it on our own—through prayer, meditation, dream study, and some creative playfulness.

AN EXERCISE FOR DESIGNING YOUR LIFE SEAL

The following is a guided imagery exercise designed to help you tune in to the wisdom of your higher self— what the readings call your individuality self. From this deeper soul level come the symbols which fill your dreams at night. In this exercise you will observe your life from the perspective of your individuality self. You will see your personality self going through a typical day. You will observe your hopes and aspirations. You will also observe the obstacles and challenges with which you are dealing right now. Near the end of the exercise you will return to your personality self with two symbols. One will represent a key ambition or goal which you currently have. The other will symbolize a central challenge which you desire to overcome.

While participating in the following exercise, keep in mind that images are more than just mental pictures. Your feelings and thoughts are just as important as the visual images. Be aware of the words, ideas, or feelings you may experience during this exercise as they *all* are important in developing your personal symbol vocabulary.

You can either have someone read this exercise to you or perhaps, even better, tape record the exercise using your *own* voice.

To begin, just relax. Sit or lie comfortably in a quiet space where you won't be disturbed for the next ten or fifteen minutes. Just close your eyes. Try to put aside any thoughts or concerns which might distract you. Focus on your breathing. Just observe the flow of air as your lungs expand to receive it. Observe the relaxation as you exhale, releasing the breath back to its source. As you inhale, imagine that you are breathing in peace and clarity. And as you exhale, release all tension and worry. So with every breath you become more and more relaxed. With every breath you become more and more quiet . . . more and more serene . . . more and more at peace. Feel yourself resting in the arms of that peace. You are relaxed . . . serene . . . quiet . . . at peace.

From this state, imagine that you are lying in your bed on a quiet, sunlit morning. Your pillow is soft. The air is fresh and clean. And all you hear is the occasional song of a morning bird. On this pleasant morning you drift in and out of sleep. And in that drowsy state you begin to feel yourself rising off the bed and drifting up into the sky. You float like a balloon, feeling the air gently lifting you higher and higher. You feel completely safe and embraced. You float toward a billowy white cloud which is slowly sailing by. As you pass, you grab onto it and climb aboard. The cloud feels like soft cotton. You nestle in and peer over the side of the cloud, to the world below. The sun feels warm on your back. And the clear air is very sweet.

From this high place you feel spiritually lifted also. You feel removed from the distractions and concerns of your daily routine. You feel a closeness to the creator and spiritual director of all life. You feel in touch with the wisdom of your higher self. Resting on a side of this cloud, looking over the landscape below, you begin to see with an inner vision. In your mind's eye you can see yourself lying in the bed from which you rose. You see yourself sleeping peacefully in your own bed. From your clear, high perspective on the cloud, you feel a love and compassion for that person lying in the bed. You understand that person's feelings. You empathize with that person's hopes and challenges. You love that person and want to help in any way you can to actualize its highest aspirations. Take a moment to feel that love and support for your own mortal self, lying in the bed far below you.

As you lie on your cloud, observing yourself on the earth, you begin to see different scenes of that person's daily activities. You observe, as through a telescope, many of the different projects that the person has undertaken. You notice that for each area of activity the person has a slightly different hat, role, or personality that it wears. In fact, the person that you observe is your personality self, a collection of many different subpersonalities, each one fitting into a certain area of life. Begin to observe your personality self as it moves from one area of life to another. Perhaps one subpersonality is involved with a relationship. Perhaps another is connected to a job. Another may be concerned with an area of personal growth.

Take a moment and from your high, detached, loving position on the cloud observe your personality self as it adapts to the different duties and responsibilities which comprise daily life. Notice which two or three areas seem to be the most important to that person right now. From your cloud you can see clearly the issues and concerns which are prominent and important to your personality self at this time. You can see clearly its desires, objectives, goals, and aspirations. You can also see distinctly the challenges and obstacles with which the person is dealing. The challenges may be located in outer circumstances. They may be inner challenges, such as a negative attitude or habit.

You release the images from your mind and roll over on the cloud so that your face is warmed by the sun. The cloud is soft and cozy, and as your higher self, you ponder for a moment what you've just seen. You reflect on the desires and the obstacles which your subpersonalities are juggling at this time . . . Lying there on your cloud, far from the hustle and bustle of daily routine, you choose one central, positive aspiration which your personality self holds at this time in life. And you also identify one chief obstacle, or challenge, which seems to divert the accomplishment of this goal. Take time now to identify those two primary components which have recently been engaging your personality self.

As you float on the cloud, warming your face in the sun, you feel a desire to *give* something to your personality self which will help it to understand its obstacle, and something to help achieve its principal aspiration. Your desire to help puts you in closer contact with the spiritual forces of love. You feel the presence of love and wisdom all around you. It seems that unseen angelic forces have joined you on the cloud and are encouraging and inspiring you. You feel that if you can get quite enough, you will receive something from these loving forces which will later give your personality self both understanding and strength. You sit up, leaning against a tuft of cloud and rest your eyes against its pure, soft whiteness.

Thinking first of the obstacle which you observed, something begins to take shape against the whiteness of the cloud. It is an image which seems to relate to that issue in your mind. You cannot make it out at first, and you have no preconceptions of what it is. When it finally becomes clear, you may be somewhat surprised to see it. Take a moment now to allow this symbol of the challenge to present itself to you . . . You reach out and take the symbol and set it beside you on the cloud.

Then you think of the central aspiration which was carried by your personality self. You again feel the presence of unseen angels in the closeness of the divine spirit embracing you. And, resting your eyes again on the whiteness of the cloud, a new symbol begins to form in your mind. It will represent the love, desire, and aspiration which your personality self holds most dear. You sit patiently as this new symbol begins to materialize. And again you may be somewhat surprised to discover what it is. Wait now and allow this image to form . . . Now you reach out and take this symbol also and set it beside you. You feel a tremendous sense of love and support and peace. You silently thank the spiritual forces of love which have surrounded you, helped you, and given you these symbols. And as you reflect on this gratitude you feel the clouds slowly lowering.

You feel that you are returning to the earth. Yet you keep with you the two symbols which you received. The cloud gently returns you to your bed, where you are re-united with your personality self. The two symbols are left with you as the cloud reascends, leaving you peace-fully in your bed. As you awaken from this experience, you take one more look at the two symbols which you acquired on the cloud. You commit them to memory as the scene slowly fades. And you become aware again of your breathing. You feel the gentle flow of air that enters and exits your lungs . . . You feel very refreshed and vital-ized as you become aware again of your body in this time and space. And when you are ready, you can open your eyes.

Now take time to reflect upon your experience. Jot down the primary pictures, thoughts, and feelings you remember. What is the symbol of aspiration from your individuality self? What is the symbol of your current challenge?

One man who followed this exercise received from his creative imagination a computer disk as one of the sym-bols. Interpreting this symbol, the man later realized that both his sense of purpose and some of his most enjoy-able moments were realized at his computer. It was there he could enter his private world of ideas and write. The disk *also* recalled for him images of the phonograph records of his early boyhood. It reminded him of similar experiences when his little record player carried him into a private world of ideas and enjoyment.

The second symbol which he received from his higher self was an ambulance. He quickly recognized this as a symbol of his current life challenge. Like an ambulance, his life had been extremely rushed and hurried. He also sensed that the symbol carried a warning for him to be careful of his health. However, the ambulance also conveyed a reference to healing, which he interpreted as an encouragement to be of service to others.

My most recent personal symbol is the seahorse. Shortly before moving to Virginia Beach and joining the staff at A.R.E., I found a seahorse on the beach while I was attending a conference on "Discovering Your Mission in Life." This little creature symbolized the strength and serenity I feel from being near the ocean. To someone else, it may mean a balance of male and female since the male horse carries its young and provides nurturing that is usually associated with the female of most species. In any event, the seahorse is at the center of my life seal, and I feel it is a very special message sent to me by the Creator since it's a rare find along the Virginia beaches.

As you can see, symbols extend in meaning to deeper and deeper levels. The more you contemplate a symbol, the more meaning it may reveal to you:

> As with those emblems then may there be chosen that which may be helpful in the experience of the entity, and may there be given that which will bring that peace, that harmony in the experiences through this sojourn, that will make as the cup upon the cross *overrunning* with what will be as pearls of wisdom in the minds and hearts of those whom the entity may contact. (1246-2)

CREATING YOUR PERSONAL LIFE SEAL

When Cayce described life seals in his readings, he was able to draw from an extremely deep level of soul awareness. Many of the symbols referred to in his readings spoke of the person's history and destiny which spanned lifetimes, as emphasized in the following reading:

In the beginning, we would give what might be said to be the seal of life for this entity. For this entity is among those that chose definite activities in the Egyptian experience, when there were those activities there for re-establishing the relationship of Creative Forces (or God) to the relationships of man. The entity was among those in the Temple Beautiful aiding those that were dedicating their lives to the activity chosen; not only in vocation but in activities through the body and mind. Hence the seal would come very close to that indicated for the entity in that experience:

In the center of a plaque or card, about fourteen inches square, make a circle about twelve to thirteen inches. This would be made in many circles, down to a point in the center. Then across each side of this connect with a vine, that would blossom upon either side right and left, at the top.

Upon this sign or vine put the honeybee; one on either side, one on wing as toward the center—indicating the varied cycles through which individuals passed, as well as how each activity in an experience—as each life in its activity—is associated or connected with the other.

The bee represents the worker, either of body, mind, or soul of the individual entity. They each have their attributes and their experience in same,

yet one—even as the manifestations in the material
experience—Father, Son, and Holy Spirit. (3377-1)

Yet, life seals can be equally valid and useful if they
address more immediate needs and issues—symbols
that relate to opportunities and challenges going on *in
this moment*. In addition to the symbols you discovered
in the reverie, the following will enable you to identify
symbols that are important to your soul growth at the
present time:

1. One or two symbols may be very logical choices
based on what you know of the symbol and how it related to your life right now.

2. However, choose at least one symbol that has an
air of mystery about it. You may not know exactly why it
is an important symbol. Perhaps it appears frequently in
your dreams or in your waking life. Perhaps it simply affects you in a strong way. Yet, you're still not sure what it
symbolizes.

3. Pick one symbol that indicates a challenge currently before you. However, when you determine the size
and arrangement of the symbols, keep this one small
and manageable. Your life seal is intended to be a visual
affirmation of hope and expectancy.

4. At least one symbol should convey the *promise of
success and fulfillment*. When arranging the symbols,
this one should be prominent—in size and/or position.
It represents your destination, your hope, your ideal.

Arrange your symbols in a circle, choose a size that
you would be most comfortable working in. It could be
as small as six inches or as big as you desire. Just keep in
mind that it's important to hang your life seal in a prominent location to stimulate your soul's development.
Choose a size accordingly.

The life seal can either be sketched as a whole or the
individual symbols can be sketched and then placed

upon the circle. Remember the circle represents completeness; and the symbols included in your life seal are meant to encourage you to come to a state of completeness—either in your journey as a whole or in solving a current problem.

Before you commit to a final design, you may want to "sleep on it" or spend some time in mediation reflecting upon the accuracy of your choices.

Cayce often suggested that a person find a friend who is artistically gifted to produce the final rendering. However, the very act of creating your own personal life seal is very powerful. It can help integrate the meaning of the symbols, both as a whole and individually, into the very core of your being, and may in fact bring about quicker spiritual development.

PART TWO:
SYMBOLS—SOME MEANINGS

There is always an air of mystery to a symbol. It comes to reveal knowledge, to stretch our understanding. Because that meaning comes from deep within the soul mind, a symbol is always far richer than what we can immediately grasp with our logical, rational minds.

In spite of the inherent limitations of a conscious mind trying to decipher the meaning of an image coming from the unconscious, it's worth the effort and certain tools may help. In Chapter Two, you've already learned how to apply the symbol amplification techniques and the symbol dialogue method. Another useful approach can sometimes be a symbol dictionary or a symbol resource guide such as appears here as Part Two of this book.

It's important to keep in mind, however, that any sort of symbol dictionary should be only a *starting point*. It's a good way of getting the pump primed, of getting your creative insights flowing.

The symbols for which interpretations are offered have been categorized into four sections, each occupying a chapter. Many of the interpretations come straight from a Cayce reading, and in those instances the reading number is noted in parenthesis. Other interpretations come from a wide variety of symbology books that were consulted in compiling this resource guide.

Don't use the ideas in Chapters Four through Seven as the final word on the meaning of a symbol. Instead, let the material in Part Two be a handy *resource* that you can turn to whenever you need a little help getting started. Ultimately, you'll probably want to create your own symbol dictionary, one that documents the association *you've* discovered for particular symbols.

Chapter 4

SHAPES AND NUMBERS

Hence all of this is given in form, ritual, the emblems, what we may term numerology, astrology, and all the forms of the ancient wisdoms; yet it is represented by the activities of same upon a physical being. (281-33)

Symbols appear in a variety of forms—numbers, color, sounds, smells, complex graphics, visions of past lives, or in simple human gestures. To fully understand a symbol's meaning, we must take into account not only its connotation within our personal experiences, but we must also explore exotic and esoteric meanings held within cultures worldwide and across history.

David Fontana, author of *The Secret Language of Symbols*, says, "The 'Christian' symbol of the cross was used by the Assyrians to represent the sky god, Anu, and by the Chinese as a symbol of the earth." He further explains that the Spaniards found crosses in the native temples in Mexico, which represented the gods Tlaloc and Quetzalcoatl. The Spaniards, however, "concluded that it had been carried to the Toltecs on a mission conducted by Saint Thomas, the legendary apostle of all the Indies."

SACRED GEOMETRY

Most graphic symbols are formed from the circle, the straight line, and the semi-circle. From these simplest forms to the ornate manifestations of the cross and other complex designs, symbolic shapes speak to us in a way that words cannot. Very often these symbols represent divine energy, and our connection with the Creator and also other forces within the universe.

 The circle—this is a figure, a symbol of completeness; as indicated by the words, "The Lord thy God is One!" [Mark 12:29] (2174-2)

According to Violet Shelley, author of *Symbols and the Self*, "The circle represents the superconscious mind, perfect and complete *before* creation. It is the symbol of unmanifested Deity, including everything and wanting nothing, without beginning or end, neither first nor last, timeless, sexless, absolute.

"In early Christian remains," Shelley adds, "the circle frequently appears as a serpent with its tail in its mouth."

 The yin/yang symbol often associated with Chinese culture and art is a depiction of the balance between the opposites of the universe—male and female energies, light and dark, good and evil, etc.

 According to Shelley, a "dot within a circle represents the center of infinity, the first cause . . . Sometimes appearing as a tiny circle within the circle, it expresses the mystic center, the original Oneness."

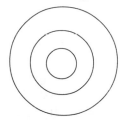

Concentric circles, with one circle inside another, represents the cosmos.

Other circular images are found in mandalas. Cayce believed that past experiences, both incarnate and discarnate, were the cause for mandalas to appear in our dreams. Elsie Sechrist, author of *Dreams—Your Magic Mirror,* says, "The most common mandalas or designs are those representing the Higher Self. This process of integration can often be seen in the abstract doodlings of a spiritually oriented individual . . . In dreams, it may be represented as a flower growing out of a pot. The process of integration is also seen as a cross within a circle, a circle within a circle, or a dot within a circle. The circle is basically a sign of wholeness."

Carl Jung painted his first mandala in 1916, but it wasn't until several years later that he began to understand the role these small circular drawings or paintings played in the development of the psyche.

"I sketched every morning in a notebook a small circular drawing, mandala, which seemed to correspond to my inner situation at the time. With the help of these drawings I could observe my psychic transformations from day to day," he writes in *Memories, Dreams, Reflections.* "When I began drawing the mandalas, however, I saw that everything, all the paths I had been following, all the steps I had taken, were leading back to a single point—namely, to the mid-point. It became increasingly

plain to me that the mandala is the centre. It is the expo-
nent of all paths. It is the path to . . . individuation."

"The circle with quaternary is the symbol
of the earth. We see that the four radii
present infinite manifestation from the
center," writes Shelley. "Familiar groups of
four represent the same ideas; the four fixed signs of the
zodiac, the four wheels in the Book of Ezekial, the four
beasts in The Revelation, the four corners of the earth,
the four seasons, the four winds, and the four elements—fire, earth, air, and water."

The semi-circle is associated with the
feminine and the subconscious. Accord-
ing to Shelley, "The crescent moon and the cup have the
same symbolic meaning as the semi-circle." The crescent moon also represents change—think of the stages
of the moon.

As the sun, the moon, the stars would be given
for signs, for seasons, for days, for years in man's
experience, then—it would not be amiss that these
would indicate the symbols as they were represented in those stages or phases of experience in
the earth. (288-50)

The triangle symbolizes the sacred trinity.
Fontana says, "Pointing upward, the triangle
stands for ascent to heaven, fire, the active
male principle: reversed, it symbolizes grace
descending from heaven, waters, the pas-
sive feminine element."
Sechrist states that "The triangle within
the circle shows the same union with the divine self; for
the triangle is representative of man in the earth and the

circle symbolizes God. Combined, it shows wholeness of ideals and purposes."

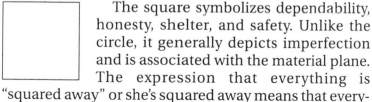

The square symbolizes dependability, honesty, shelter, and safety. Unlike the circle, it generally depicts imperfection and is associated with the material plane. The expression that everything is "squared away" or she's squared away means that everything is all set. Reference to a square meal means a balanced meal.

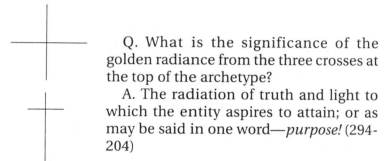

Q. What is the significance of the golden radiance from the three crosses at the top of the archetype?

A. The radiation of truth and light to which the entity aspires to attain; or as may be said in one word—*purpose!* (294-204)

While usually associated with Christianity, the cross has meanings from different historical periods as well as cultures. While all symbols are meant to evoke a response, perhaps this is most evident with the cross, which is meant to remind us of our connection with the Divine. Shelley says it is to remind us of both the descent of spirit into matter and also of our "way out . . . This, of course, makes it the perfect symbol of agony, struggle, and martyrdom."

In the following reading, Cayce suggested that the person [2029] wear the cross to raise her vibration:

A Maltese cross of teakwood should be worn by the entity at all times, next to the skin, about the neck or waist . . . this would have a helpful influence by creating a *vibration*. Not that it would within itself have an influence, but the associations of same would become as helpful influences—just as that you think gradually grows to become *you*— as you digest its influence or force. (2029-1)

Cayce often recommended that a person keep a symbol, such as a stone, with particular personal meaning within sight or on the body. By the very wearing of the cross, Cayce is suggesting that this person's vibrations will be heightened—"as you digest its influence or force."

The swastika, another form of a cross, is found in many cultures and represents both male and female energy. It has particular relevance with the Jains, the Buddhists, and followers of Vishnu. Shelley says it was found in ancient Troy and among the Mayas, and "its form suggests movement through life." (The Nazis used a reverse form of the swastika to symbolize their philsophy.)

The cross is oftentimes combined with the circle. The ankh, also known as the Key of Life, is associated with ancient Egypt. Shelley says, "As a cross, it has the same meaning as the Latin cross. The almost circular handle is a symbol of higher planes. The handle is not a perfect circle, but elongated, indicating that when the soul enters upon the limitations of the cycle of life (the zodiac) it is no longer wholly divine."

Here Cayce describes a meaning associated with the combination of the circle and the cross:

Q. What is the sign of His presence?
A. The circle with the cross; these make for the

sign that all thou hast heard is fulfilled in Him. (423-3)

The ankh is similar to the Celtic cross, which is said to depict the union of heaven and earth.

The cross with the serpent, according to Shelley, "indicates man's necessity to rise above his desirous nature [in order for the spirit to work its way back to its source]. Man, standing with feet together and arms outstretched, is himself in the shape of the cross. It is truly in the flesh that the spirit of God is crucified."

The Tau cross, taken from "the ideographic symbols in the Chinese language, shows the spiritual principle in near equilibrium with the principle of the world of phenomena," Shelley says. "It is a symbol of the manifestation of the spiritual."

The inverted Tau cross shows the process of evolution, of spirit ascending from matter. It is also said to represent humility.

The pentagram, a five-pointed star known as the star of the Magi, is believed to have the ability to ward off negativity. Sechrist states that "Cayce suggested that it represents man's experiences in the earth through his five senses."

The Seal of Solomon or Star of David is associated with Judaism. According to Kevin Todeschi, author of *The Encyclopedia of Symbolism*, "the six points of the two interwoven triangles represent the six days of Creation." Other sources suggest that these triangles symbolize the harmonious connection of masculine and feminine energy within the universe. It can also represent humankind's journey from God or the Source and also its return.

Todeschi says that the pyramid is "symbolic of the spirit (the pinnacle of the structure) manifesting into the earth (the four corners of the base)" and "often associated with ancient wisdom or spiritual initiation."

SYMBOLIC MEANINGS OF NUMBERS

There are many references in Scripture to numbers; not for their quantitative measure, but more for their symbolic meanings. Cayce, too, refers to the symbology of numbers in his readings:

> Each individual vibrates to certain numbers according to his name, his birthdate, and his relationships to various activities. When numbers appear, they represent strength or weakness, assets or deterrents, change or stability. They are also signs or omens. They may be used as warnings or as aids in any manner helpful to the individual. (5751-1)

One. Shelley says, "*One* reminds us of the one God, the one Life, the oneness of mankind, the power of Selfhood; of self-reliance, dignity, rulership; the wand of the magician, the rod of power, the power of will."

One is the beginning, to be sure. Before *One* is nothing. After *One* is nothing, if all be *in One*—as

One God, *One* Son, *One* Spirit. This, then, the *essence* of *all* force, *all* manners of energies. All activities *emanate* from the *One*. (5751-1)

As in numbers one builds upon the other (as units) and all are formations or divisions or multiples of units of one, so the universe and the expressions of all natures within same are the manifestations of that one force, one power, one spirit, one energy known as Universal Force, Creative Energy, or God. (1462-1)

In numerology, which is based on the Pythagorean system, one signifies new beginnings, individuality, and creativity.

Two. According to Shelley, "As the number One represents Adam, so the number Two symbolizes Adam and Eve, man and woman, the masculine and feminine aspects of the Creative Force manifesting in human form; for form can result only from the interaction of the positive and negative poles."

Two—the *combination*, and begins a division of the Whole, or the One. While *two* makes for strength, it *also* makes for weakness. This is *illustrated* in that of your music, of your paintings, of your metals, of *whatever* element we may consider! (5751-1)

Two also represents the balance between polarities within the universe.

Three. Cayce said that odd numbers held more strength than even numbers because they always contain one.

Three—again a combination of One and Two; this making for strength, making for—in division—

that ability of Two against One, or One *against* Two. In *this* strength is seen, as in the Godhead, and is as a greater strength in the whole of combinations. (5751-1)

The trinity is represented in the number three, as well as the body, mind, and spirit. It indicates a time of self-expression and expansion.

Four. Like the square, the number four stands for stability and materiality. Todeschi states that it "may also represent the four seasons, the four winds, the four elements (air, earth, fire, and water), the four Gospels, or the Four Horsemen of the Revelation.

Again, in *Four*, we find that of a division—and while a beauty in strength, in the divisions also makes for the greater weakness—as may be illustrated as in the combinations seen in metal, or numbers, or music, or color. (5751-1)

Five. According to Denise Linn, author of *The Secret Language of Signs*, "Five is the number of the free soul, of excitement and change." Cayce emphasizes the association of change with the number five in the following:

Five—as seen, a change—as may be seen in a comparison of any of the forces outlined. (5751-1)

Six. "Six is the number of the Christ-force in nature. It represents balance or ambivalence. It corresponds to the cessation of movement, since creation took six days," writes Shelley. "The number stands for intuition, harmony, and beauty, and love that has gone from passionate to compassionate. It is a symbol of accomplishment, growth, and purpose."

Compassion is a necessary component of community service, and hence six may indicate a need to be of service to humankind or to be a contributing member of your community.

Cayce stated that six refers to beauty and strength, as he emphasized in the following reading:

> Six—again makes for the *beauty* and the symmetrical forces of *all numbers,* making for strength . . . (5751-1)

Seven. Seven is indicative of a spiritual path, perhaps one of solitude and contemplation. Here is Cayce's description of this number:

> As does *Seven* signify the *spiritual* forces, as are seen in all the ritualistic orders of any nature; as seen in the dividing up of conditions, whether they be of the forces in nature or those that react to the sensual forces of man in any character. (5751-1)

According to Shelley seven "is the most sacred of all numbers. . ." It is symbolic of perfect order, a complete period or cycle. It is the number of the basic series of musical notes, the colors in the spectrum, the planetary spheres, the endocrine glands, or spiritual centers in the body."

Eight. The figure eight, similar in shape to the infinity symbol, could signify abundance and the endless nature of divine consciousness. In the following reading, Cayce emphasizes the attributes of strength and weakness when referring to this number:

> *Eight*—again showing that combination in strength, also a combination in weakness. (5751-1)

Shelley says, "The numeral Eight, because of its shape, is associated with the two interlacing serpents of the caduceus, signifying, therefore, the pattern of movement of creative energy . . . It is the symbol of regeneration and the entrance into a new state or condition of the soul."

Nine. Nine indicates completion, an ending of a cycle. In *The Encyclopedia of Symbols*, Todeschi says it "may be symbolic of compassion, universality, selflessness, or truth. " This concurs with Cayce's description as set forth in the following:

> *Nine* making for the *completeness* in numbers; yet showing not the strength as of Ten, nor yet the weakness as of Eight, yet making for that termination in the *forces* in natural *order* of things that come as a change in the imminent in the life. (5751-1)

Shelley writes that it is "the number of the initiate" and has "been considered the number of mystery. It is sometimes symbolized by the mystic rose, which is represented in a stylized form with nine petals on the outer edge, six in the next row, and three around the center."

Here Cayce referred to the importance of the numbers three, six, and nine for a forty-five-year-old woman:

> And let the numbers as in three, six, and nine ever be the choice, whether in the activities in the material, in the sojourn, in the position, in the place, or in *whatever* the activities may be; for these carry with them their vibration by the *natural* relative forces to the human emotions. (694-2)

Ten. Todeschi writes that ten "corresponds to a return to unity" and that it "may represent that which is human (i.e., ten fingers and ten toes)." Cayce refers to this number as symbolizing completeness:

> In *Ten* we have those of the completeness as of
> numbers, and a strength as is found in *few;* yet these
> are as a combination in the forces as are manifest.
> (5751-1)

"The Egyptian priests placed great importance on the number Ten, and before offering the sacrifice fasted and conformed to a rigid discipline for ten days," writes Shelley in *Symbols and the Self.* "Among the Hindus, the number Ten is referred to as a magic power. The cipher represents man's vast unmanifested nature, which is worth nothing until he uses the Rod of Power—his divine creative spirit. Among the Masons, the number Ten is a sign of union and good faith expressed by joined hands."

Eleven. Numerologists consider eleven to be one of the master numbers and it symbolizes mastery on the physical plane. It is also associated with courage, power, spirituality, enlightenment, spiritual healing, and intuition. Twenty-two and thirty-three are also master numbers. Twenty-two is a number symbolizing mastery of the mental realm; and thirty-three, mastery of the spiritual.

> In *Eleven* is again seen those of the *beauty* of
> numbers, yet that weakness as was signified by
> those of the betrayal in the numbers. (5751-1)

Twelve. In addition there are twelve months to the year, and twelve astrological houses, represented in the Wheel of Life which is divided into twelve segments. "Here the original circle of Divine Manifestation is marked off into twelve equal divisions by the fourfold expression of the Divinity (the triangle) within it," says

Shelley. "The wheel embodies the idea of rotation, and the spokes radiating from the hub express spirit in manifestation. The twelve divisions of the cycle of life may very well correspond to soul states and soul qualities."

"*Twelve* is symbolic of cosmic order, spiritual perfection, and completion. It is the number of the manifested universe and is the basis of all duodecenary groups," says Shelley. There are many references in the Bible to the number twelve: the tribes of Israel, the apostles, sons of Jacob.

Twelve—as a *finished product,* as is given in all forces nature; as was given in all forces as combined to those of the ritualistic forms, those of the mystic forces, those of the numbers as related to those of a combination; for as of the voices of *Twelve* requiring Twenty to even drown same, or to overcome same. The same as may be seen in all of the forces in nature. *Twelve* combined forces brought those strengths into the world as of [were] necessary for a replenishing of same. (5751-1)

Chapter 5

SYMBOLS OF THE PLANETS

As to the astrological aspects, we find these—as from the beginning of man's expression in materiality, through the God-given forces—are for signs and symbols, and indicate tendencies because of associations or affiliation of the entity in that particular environ. (1791-1)

Each of the planets has both attributes and detriments, as well as mental patterns associated with each. Cayce frequently spoke of these planetary influences in aura chart readings, giving directions for the placement of astrological symbols.

"These were meant to indicate the plane of consciousness from which the entity entered an incarnation, or to which he went after a life in the earth," writes Violet Shelley in *Symbols and the Self.*

She further states: "Mental urges and abilities are the result of preparation between earth lives." Cayce suggested that the soul manifests in material form only in the earth, thus resulting in our emotional nature. This is explained in the following reading:

In the applications of those that are experiences in the earth, these are as the emotional or the sense emotions of the material experience; while indwellings in the environs of the astrological sojourns between those periods of material or earthly activity are as innate urges and are the greater influence when those urges from the atomic forces of such an influence are more perceptible by their position— and when the greater number of sojourners in such an environment are banded in a material activity. Yet all of these are, as indicated, but as urges; and what one does with one's experience, knowledge, or understanding, makes for that which is the advancement or the retardment. For each soul must meet *itself* and *its* activity *in the earth;* whether in a particular or individual sojourn or in *whatever* the activity may be. For Life is *One!* And what ye sow ye *must* also reap. (845-1)

In the following reading Cayce described the mental urges of the planets. However, he cautioned that each of us has free will to submit to these influences as we choose.

The strongest force used in the destiny of man is the Sun first, then the closer planets to the earth, or those that are coming to ascension at the time of the birth of the individual, *but let it be understood here, no action of any planet or the phases of the Sun, the Moon or any of the heavenly bodies surpass the rule of man's will power, the* power given by the Creator of man, in the beginning, when he became a living soul, with the power of choosing for himself. (3744-4)

The following are the planetary influences that Cayce

described consistently throughout many readings:

As in Mercury pertaining of Mind.
In Mars of Madness.
In Earth as of Flesh.
In Venus as Love.
In Jupiter as Strength.
In Saturn as the beginning of earthly woes, that to which all insufficient matter is cast for the beginning.
In that of Uranus as of the Psychic.
In that of Neptune as of Mystic.
In Septimus [Pluto] as of Consciousness.
(900-10)

Ancient symbols formed from the basic graphic symbols described earlier in this book represent each of the planets. The unconscious mind or the infinite is depicted by the circle; the conscious or masculine energy, the straight line; and the unconscious or feminine energy by the semi-circle.

MERCURY

From Mercury we find the high mental abilities, and yet these may at times cause rather harsh judgments. (958-3)

Individuals with a Mercury influence tend to intellectualize and analyze situations. They have quick minds and like to get all the facts. Mercury rules Gemini and Virgo.

In Mercury we find an influence of high *mental* capacity in the individual activities towards *things*, towards conditions, rather than peoples.

For oft in the experience of the entity has the entity in this sojourn been able through the mental self to determine the motivative influence in the experience of individuals without the comprehension of that which the entity or individual has done about that it has acted with or upon. (1021-3)

In *The Encyclopedia of Symbolism*, Kevin Todeschi reports that Mercury is "symbolic of the messenger of the gods" in Roman mythology and "associated with communications, reason, and calculation."

It is also helpful to recognize the properties of mercury as a metal to gain some understanding, perhaps, of your moods, a close associate, or of a situation. Its properties include quickness, changeability, and volatility.

VENUS

In Venus we find the lovely becoming the expressions in activities in which there is the beauty seen in love, in companionship, in association, in music, in art, in *all* the things that bespeak of the *loveliness* even of nature and the material things, rather than the expression of same in the earthly form or manner. (949-13)

The attributes of Venus are love, beauty, companionship, and music, according to Todeschi.

In Venus we find the beauty, the love of romance, the love of the beautiful, the artistic temperment; that of dependency and that yet of a seeking for truth *wherever* it may be found. (1791-1)

Venus folks prefer to do things in partnership. They appreciate beauty of both places and people, and are usually very vulnerable. Venus rules Taurus and Libra.

MARS

In the urge through Mars' forces brings that at times of the temper that has been subdued in part through that of self's will to apply that of love and forbearance, rather than that as would appear in the urge to enact at that time. (165-2)

Mars is the symbol of power, creation, and dynamic energy, according to Shelley. "It can refer to anger and self-assertiveness or it can exalt these into courage, strength of character, and self-confidence."

From Mars we find the urges for activity, the intenseness with which the entity gives itself to that it chooses. Not that the entity has not also a temper of its own, and holds its grudge where it thinks it should—but no one has a right to hold any grudge. (3299-1)

In early mythology, Mars was "the god of farming, fertility, and prosperity of harvest," according to Denise

Linn, author of *The Secret Language of Signs*. As the Roman god of war, Mars "represents the small disharmonies in your life."

Mars rules Aries and Scorpio. Mars people like competition and challenges, especially those that are physically demanding. They do have a temper, however.

JUPITER

Jupiter brings the bigness of vision, the nobleness of purpose, the patience with self as well as with others. (428-4)

Jupiter's characteristics symbolize soul growth, expansion, and magnanimity. Todeschi says that it is associated with benevolence and supreme kindness.

In Jupiter we find abilities in a helpful, universal way and manner. Hence the entity is given to verboseness, as well as in abilities to depict situations, to analyze people and places, things and conditions. Thus may the entity be gifted in writing, lecturing, and in group direction. (3299-1)

Individuals with a Jupiter influence can envision the big picture. They're comfortable with power and money and enjoy philosophy. Jupiter rules Sagittarius.

SATURN

. . . from Saturn we find the influences from which there is the new beginning—ever the constant wanting to rub out and begin over again, the constant change that arises. (949-13)

Saturn rules Capricorns. These individuals are conservative, cautious, and reluctant to change, yet are often forced to do so. They are also disciplined and persistent.

In Saturn we find the sudden or violent changes—those influences and environs that do not grow, as it were, but are sudden by that of change of circumstance, materially, or by activities apparently upon the part of others that become a part of self by the very associations. And yet these are testing periods of thy endurance, of thy patience, of thy love of truth, harmony, and the spirit that faileth not. (1981-1)

URANUS

Uranian influences are for the *extremes*; very high, very low in the phases of human endeavor or human experience. In the using of same, then, as they turn to the occult or mystical forces in the experiences of individuals they tend to make for the activities in which individuals give credence to numbers, days, seasons, or become as it were superstitious to this or that form. These are manners of expression of this influence. (949-13)

Uranus folks are subject to mood swings and are often high-strung. They're also very intuitive, scientific, and inventive. Uranus rules Aquarius.

In Uranus we find the very obstinate conditions; these, as we find, make for *conflicts*. For, with the high mental abilities, what the entity knows it knows, irrespective of what others may say or think, and it smilingly goes on its merry way.

What the entity thinks or feels at times about its associations is also governed in a manner by the extreme influences from the sojourn in Uranus.

It makes also for the interest in the occult and mystic. And if there is the opportunity (and make same) for the entity in its activity to portray the actions or emotions tending towards the natures partaking of the occult forces, or the occult sources, in *such* portrayals may the entity excel in its own activity. (989-2)

NEPTUNE

Neptune is associated with mysticism, spiritual insight and development, the realization of divine love, and the vision of completion. Other qualities include clairvoyance, genius, and sensitivity. Neptune is the god of the sea in Roman mythology.

In Neptune we find both warnings and helpful forces, both virtue and vices.

Then, stay close to water. It is the mother in nature, and nothing is more beautiful than the mother's love, the mother's caress—even in anger or in disquietude. For, this influence is strong in the body-mind and consciousness of the entity. For, the entity, too, has known, has expressed and manifested mother love.

Know, too, that in the same sign there is that of violence and of anger, that of sorrow from the word spoken . . .

Weakness in the body arises also from this sign, and becomes even as the quicksands—that are neither solid nor yet water, neither possessed with that other than fear. (2448-2)

Neptune individuals are attracted to the mysterious, mystical side of life. The sea and other forces of nature hold them in awe. Neptune rules Pisces.

PLUTO

Cayce referred to Pluto as Septimus in the readings and also stated that it was the same as the planet Vulcan. Pluto signifies transformation from one level of consciousness to another, a rebirth. It is associated with the

Roman god of the underworld and could represent self-centeredness or the growth potential of an individual.

In astrological associations, these would appear adverse in their first appearance, coming much under the influence of the Dog Star and Vulcan. These make for that influence as has been of sudden changes in the social affairs, the relationships as respecting those of kinship, and those changes as respecting physical or business relations; yet these *adversities* may be used or applied . . . as stepping-stones for [the] soul's development, as well as of a mental and material change in the experience of the entity. (1727-1)

Pluto rules Scorpio. Individuals under the influence of Pluto are explosive, passionate, and self-oriented.

Chapter 6

Nature's Symbols

He who understands nature walks close with God.
(1904-2)

In *all nature* the Spirit of Creation is *emanating*, and one
that attunes self in *mind* or mental forces towards *beings*
of emanation, gains knowledge in an *inestimable* manner, that becomes the soul, the personality, the *being* of
the individual. (345-2)

Where else could the universe speak so beautifully to
us than through our natural surroundings and creatures
with whom we share this planet? In *Dreams—Your Magic
Mirror,* Elsie Sechrist says, "Trees, flowers, fruit, and
plants . . . often appear as symbols of our spiritual state.
When they look healthy, we are enjoying individual
growth; when they are dying through neglect or for lack
of water, we must search within ourselves for a spiritual
deficiency."

The entity then was among "things" and yet was
touched in person, was touched in heart, and
sought to know the meaning of same, for it saw
then fruit, leaves, trees, which had their spiritual

meaning in people's lives. (5373-1)

One woman notes that whenever she sees her plants drooping from lack of water, she knows she has also been neglecting herself and that she also needs nurturing. It usually indicated a need for her to spend more time involved in spiritual pursuits rather than material endeavors.

FLOWERS

Listen at the birds. Watch the blush of the rose. Listen at the life rising in the tree. These serve their Maker. Through what? That psychic force, that *is* Life itself . . . Learn thine lesson, O Man, from that about thee! (364-10)

Flowers in general symbolize beauty. The lotus, rose, and lily are frequently used as sun symbols, according to Shelley. Individually they also have their own meanings.

Calla lily: majestic beauty

Chrysanthemum: What conjures up an image of fall more than the chrysanthemum with all its vibrant colors.

Daffodil: new beginnings

Daisy: youth

Fleur-de-lis: freedom from oppression; also symbol for Joan of Arc and the Virgin Mary

And during a portion of those experienced the fleur-de-lis became as an emblem of security. So it may in the present bring the more of the awareness, in the very vibrations of same, of freedom, and yet the dependence of one upon another for things that may bring safety or security into the experiences of the many. (2109-2)

Garlic: the higher world

Lily: transformation, life and rebirth; Easter; purity; Cayce says this of the lily:

> As is seen, in the seemingly uncouth and un-comely herb in the muck, the root puts forth itself to obtain from this muck that which the entity sees burst forth in its beauty and fragrance. (137-63)

Lotus: represents enlightenment, higher self; a blos-soming

Mistletoe: a kiss; Christmas

Morning glory: resurrection

Pansy: humility

> As to the flowers—the pansy, in its reproduction of its vibrations from the earth, is active in such manners as to become centralizing for the entity in its meditation. (1037-1)

Rose: often thought of as a symbol of love; the Masons think of it as representing light, love, and life; the Roscrucians believe red roses symbolize Christ

> And the star with the rose upon same should be the emblem worn ever by the entity about its body,

for it will to the entity bring strength and light and hopefulness that is signified in the blooming of beauty in the light of the love in the Father. (695-1)

In referring to a five-pointed star and a rose in *one* symbol, Cayce said this:

One is the light that will guide thee. The other is the symbol of life that is ever as a sweet essence or incense before Him, guiding, unfolding in the service that thou dost give to thy fellow man. (695-1)

Shamrock: Holy Trinity; Ireland

Sunflower: joy; fullness of life

Thistle: fall of man

TREES

This, of course, would have tiny leaves and the buds may be made green and the shade green of the stem, and the tiny leaves as a different or more verdant green; while the bulbs would be silver. These would indicate the growth, and the tying together of the characteristics of the entity, as it were, as it listened in that period of the greater unfoldment. (1709-9)

Many different cultures revered trees. The Celts and Druids felt that the oak symbolized divinity and strength; the Egyptian god Osiris revered the tamarisk; and the elder, ivy, bay, and laurel were often mentioned in Greek mythology. In some Buddhist traditions the fig tree symbolizes enlightenment. Pines stand for clarity and purification. Divining rods used to detect water are made from hazel trees.

"The tree can be associated with all four elements and appears as a symbol in the metaphorical language of all the major religions," writes Shelley. "It stands for the inexhaustible life and . . . immortality . . . absolute reality."

Christmas tree: even in the dead of winter, this tree gives us hope of life, life that will return to us again in the spring

Cypress: hope

Fruit trees: a fruitful life

Oak: strength, wisdom

Palm: used in the Christian tradition at Easter, represents life after death; many of us associate palm trees with warmth and freedom (especially from long winters)

Pine: longing, as in pining for someone; peace—the negative ions of the pine tree help to calm one's emotions

Tree of Life: emblem of the Virgin Mary giving birth to Jesus, her fruit; could also represents perfect harmony and, according to Cayce, the spiritual centers of the body as referred to in the Bible: "the tree of life in the midst of the garden"

Weeping willow: sorrow

Woods/forest: confusion

The way through wood representing that maze as is presented to the mind . . . (136-16)

ANIMALS AND BIRDS

For, as seen, each animal, each bird, each fowl, has been so named for some peculiarity of that individual beast, bird, or fowl, and in this manner represents some particular phase of man's development in the earth's plane, or that consciousness of some particular element or personality that is manifested in man. (294-87)

When Cayce was questioned about the symbols of the seven stages of humanity's development, he referred to the following inhabitants of the animal and bird worlds:

The world as the beetle. Birth as the cockerel. The Mind as the serpent. Wisdom as the hawk. (281-25)

Cayce frequently made mention of animals in his readings and interpreted their meanings, especially in their appearances in dreams. He believed birds symbolized love and the thymus center.

Elsie Sechrist writes, "Birds . . . often relate to beauty, joy, and love, or that transcendent quality that lifts man from serfdom to his lower self to freedom in the expression of his high self. The symbol of a bird appears frequently in history, in the Bible, and in the dreams of men and women when they go through critical periods in their lives."

Animals frequently represent universal religious symbols. The eagle, the lion, and the ox, which appeared in Ezekiel's vision, are symbols of three of the Evangelists. Mark is represented by the lion; Luke, the ox; and John, the eagle. Three sons of the Egyptian sun god Horus are also animals. Four horses appear in The Revelation, each bearing an individual message. According to Cayce, the white horse represents the need to balance and control the sex drive; the red horse is a symbol for the adrenals or emotional center; the black horse calls for balancing of the male/female qualities in our souls; and the pale horse symbolizes the thymus gland and our affections or love.

We can learn even more from the animals and birds that cross our paths by looking to their natural habits and characteristics.

> Go to the ant, thou sluggard—understand his ways and be wise . . . They choose by their instinct. Ye learn by application of choice . . . (1965-1)

Ants are associated with patience, community, productivity, self-sacrifice, and little annoyances. Ants frequently turned up in one woman's kitchen when she was becoming impatient with the process of life. While intuitively she knew what direction she was heading or what events were about to take place, she often found it difficult to wait for the events to play out. Ants traipsing across her counter were a reminder to slow down, have faith, and let the process of life unfold.

"Ant is a builder like a Beaver, is aggressive like Badger, has stamina like Elk, scrutiny like Mouse, and giveaway like Turkey," say Jamie Sams and David Carson, authors of *Medicine Cards: The Discovery of Power Through the Ways of Animals*, adding that "Ant people are planners, like Squirrel, and are content to see their dreams being built a little at a time."

Armadillo: boundaries; armor. You may need to set some personal boundaries.

Badger: aggressiveness; anger; willingness to fight. You may need to be more aggressive in accomplishing your goals, or perhaps you are being too aggressive and pouncing on those nearby.

Bat: Are you a little batty? Are you blind as a bat? Or is the bat symbolizing your rebirth, of going into the unknown and trusting your intuition?

Bear: If bears come to your awareness, it could be a time to go within, just as the bear goes within its cave in the winter. You, too, may need to hibernate, withdraw from outward activities, in order to reflect upon a situation that may be bearing down on you. Bears can be associated with a falling stock market or with Russia.

As is seen in the character of the beast—represented by the bear: that one who would under certain conditions be very destructive, under other phases of its consciousness playful, and as caressing and as loving and as tender as protective to the best interests of the individual in every way, as much so as would any of those who come to the individual's assistance. (294-87)

Beaver: Beavers are builders and hard workers. Are you working hard, perhaps too hard or not hard enough? Beavers also possess the qualities of perseverance, adaptability, and creativity. And when building their lodges, they always leave themselves an escape route. This could signify the need for you not to paint yourself into a corner with some situation.

Bee: Are you busy as a bee? Perhaps you need to just be. Have you been stung by someone or some situation? Also represent obstacles to overcome.

Beetles: signs of good luck and abundance. Ancient Egyptians believed the beetle symbolized eternal life and rebirth.

Bird: messenger; also symbol of the soul

> ... just as the bird manifests the messenger to the
> peoples ... (900-37)

Bluebirds: good luck, happiness, joy

Boars: associated with aggression and ferociousness;
or perhaps someone (yourself?) is boring.

> ... as the boar the destructive destruction, or
> gormandizing of self in indulgences ... (1931-1)

Buffalo: may indicate a tendency to "buffalo" or intimi-
date others; perhaps a desire to be wild and roam free.
The Native Americans used the buffalo for food, clothing, and shelter, so a buffalo could mean that your needs
will be met; could indicate a time to pray for whatever
you need.

Bug: Is something bugging you, or are you bugging
someone?

Bull: bull-headed; our animal nature; rising stock market
    It's interesting to note that sacrificing the bull, which
has been prevalent throughout history, symbolizes "the
victory of man's spiritual nature over his animality—of
which the bull is a common symbol," according to Jung.

Butterfly: transformation and change; joy and bliss. Are
you a social butterfly?

Cat: independence, being catty. Are you prone to gos-
sip?

Chickens: could be associated with fear or timidity. Or you've been perhaps fluttering about, like a "chicken with its head cut off." If you dream of a *rooster*, perhaps you're being cocky or aggressive; or are you being hen-pecked?

Cockroaches: irritation; unclean

Coyote: trickster; self-sabotage. It could mean that you're fooling yourself.

Crab: Are you being crabby and irritable? Do you have a hard shell, which prevents people from approaching you? Astrologically associated with one sign of the zodiac—Cancer.

Crocodiles: harsh words, biting remarks; false tears

Crow: protector; keeper of sacred law in Native American tradition; could signify change

Deer: gentleness, kindness; may be a warning not to push for something in your life; take a gentler approach to a problem. May also represent money.

Dogs: faithfulness, loyalty, and unconditional love. The Native Americans considered dogs to be the symbol of service. Within the community, dogs provided protection, often warning of impending danger. They also served as loyal friends to their masters, even in the face of harsh treatment.

> Those who are as friendly as a dog to man . . .
> (294-94)

One woman frequently dreamt of dogs and through

her work in a dream/therapy group realized their symbolic significance. To her dogs represented her instincts.
Whenever she dreamt of dogs she analyzed whether or
not she was trusting her instincts or her intuitions.

> One in the form of the dog (which represents a
> certain nature, character, or disposition of an indi-
> vidual—which may not always be trusted) . . . (294-
> 87)

Dogs also have negative connotations. They can be
aggressive and territorial and are known to turn on their
owners. Laziness is referred to in the phrase "It's a dog's
life." And when someone's in the dog house, it usually
means they're in trouble.

Dolphin: keeper of the sacred breath; peace; communication between species (or one another); spiritual wisdom or intuition

Donkey: stubbornness; heavy loads; humility. Are you
being an "ass" about some situation?

Dove: peace, tranquillity, hope; new life; Holy Spirit

Duck: Are you avoiding (ducking) an issue? Are you
comfortable in some situation (like a duck takes to water)?

Eagle: symbol of the creator, especially for Native
Americans. In ancient Egypt it symbolized illumination.
It can also symbolize the need to take a look at a situation from high above. Give yourself the freedom to soar
above your earthly connections. True wise love, freedom
with responsibility.

Elephant: power, strength; good memory

   The elephant as represents the power, might, cunning, with all the mental proclivities of that gained through knowledge. (341-15)

Elk: stamina, strength; may be a warning to pace yourself, especially if life has you burning the candles at both ends

Fish: Is something fishy going on? Are you feeling like a fish out of water, uncomfortable with some situation? Also represents faith; spirituality, and Christ.

Fox: crafty, clever, and cunning. Also adaptability, observation, swiftness of thought and action. A fox crossing your path could indicate that it's time for you to sit quietly and observe your surroundings, perhaps blend in and be unseen. Could also mean sexy.

Frog: Could indicate a time for cleansing, perhaps with tears or by clearing your calendar and spending some time alone; sign of stillness, patience, focus; Madame Blavatsky says the frog symbolized creation and resurrection. Kevin Todeschi, in *The Encyclopedia of Symbolism*, suggests that it could also indicate you have difficulty speaking (having a frog in your throat), or that there are hurdles to leap over.

Giraffes: ability to see from above; or a distortion (as in the neck); could also symbolize a throat ailment or something that is out of reach.

Goldfish: something valuable; spiritual insight

Goose: silliness

Hawk: messenger of God; signifies a time when we must be aware of the messages from our Creator, a time to heighten our awareness

Hornet: irritation; problems; being stung by a situation or person; obstacles to overcome

Horse: power and freedom; for many cultures, the horse provided ease of transportation. Native Americans believed the horse allowed them to travel to the inner realms. Cayce described the horse as a messenger in The Revelation.

Hummingbird: joy, opening the heart, harmony and energy

Ladybug: good luck, protection; sign of new things to come

Lamb: purity, innocence, meekness, Christ; are you being sacrificed, or is this a time to be unassuming?

Lion: majesty, power, bravery, leadership—is it time to take control? Jung felt it symbolized our latent passions. Is your courage being tested, like the cowardly lion in *The Wizard of Oz?*

Lizard: symbolizes the importance of dreaming

Lynx: knower of secrets; may indicate a time to notice the visions or mental images you are receiving in your dreams or while awake

Mockingbird: Are you mocking something or some-one? Are you forgetting your individuality?

Monkey: mischief, frivolity

Moose: self-esteem; strength and pride

Mountain lion: leadership and responsibility; a time to stand up for your convictions and tell the truth.

Mouse: scrutiny; may indicate a time to look more closely at your life and surroundings

Octopus: the number eight; attachment; do you have your hands in too many projects? Also represents the unfolding of creation.

Opossum: a diversion; are you playing dead to creatively avoid a confrontation?

Otter: female qualities of our souls; playfulness, curiosity

Owl: represents transformation, death, and rebirth; wisdom; also could mean deception; may indicate a need to be observant so that you are not deceived.

Peacock: eternal life; pride—are you as proud as a peacock, perhaps too proud?

Pets: Pets very often take on the energy of their owners. If your pet is ill, it could be a warning to watch your own health; if he or she is acting neurotic, perhaps you need to meditate on the opportunities you are facing.

Pig: greed, being a "hog"

Porcupine: innocence; trust and faith; also could mean defensiveness

Phoenix: transformation; radiant energy; intuition; sudden change

Rabbit: reproduction; Easter or awakening; fear or worry; could also indicate a need or a habit of burrowing

Rat: destruction; disease; unkind

Raven: God's love; God as the source of the supply for all our needs; change of consciousness

Robin: spring, new beginnings

Scorpion: danger; poison; stinging

Shark: aggressiveness; treacherous; unexpected attacks; if you think of a card shark, could you be cheated or are you cheating?

Skunk: reputation, self-respect; it could be time to walk your talk and be proud of your accomplishments; something that is repelling

Snake: temptation; rising kundalini forces; sneakiness or danger. Since snakes shed their skins, it could indicate a time of transmutation or change of the body, mind, or soul; also wisdom.

Spider: weaver, web, infinite possibilities. Are you limiting yourself or are you becoming caught in a web of deceit?

Squirrel: Squirrels often exhibit erratic behavior as they scurry from tree to tree. They also signify preparation, perhaps for something as normal as the change in seasons or perhaps a major life change. It could indicate that you are dealing with your shadow side.

Swan: grace and beauty; intuition and awareness

> The swans as representing peace and serenity . . .
> (262-8)

Tadpole: As indicated, this represents the beginning.
(294-204)

Turkey: spirit of giving and sharing

Turtle: Native Americans often refer to North America
as Turtle Island; also a symbol for Mother Earth; protection; motherly compassion.
     When you stumble upon one, could it mean that
you've been hiding in your shell and that it's time to
come out? Or perhaps it's time to go within and shelter
yourself from the world for a time. It was also the turtle
that won the race, so slow and steady may be the pace
for you.
     Cayce believed it stood for long life or a new life, and
strength.

Vulture: death; also protection and maternal care

Weasel: energy, ingenuity, observation

Whale: ancient knowledge, soul history; could indicate
a need for you to use toning exercises to bring balance to
your emotional and physical body

Wolf: strong family and community ties; teacher; may
indicate a time to connect with your inner wisdom and
sharing what you've learned

Chapter 7

The Symbolism of Our Bodies and Our Environments

He has promised to meet thee within the temple of thine own body. For as has been given, thy body is the temple of the living God; a tabernacle, yea, for the soul. And in the holy of holies within thine own consciousness He may walk and talk with thee. (987-4)

Our bodies are miniature replicas of the universe. This is reflected in many symbolic phrases such as "as above, so below." Carolyn Myss, noted medical intuitive and author of *Anatomy of the Spirit*, says, "The Book of Genesis describes Adam's body as created 'in the image of God.' The message in this phrase is both literal and symbolic. It means that people are energy duplicates of a Divine power—a system of seven primary energies whose truths we are meant to explore and develop through this experience called life." These energy centers are the chakras which correlate to the seven endocrine glands within the body.

OUR ACHES, PAINS, AND AILMENTS

Louise L. Hay, author of *You Can Heal Your Life*, has identified emotional patterns that affect different areas of our bodies. "The body, like everything else in life, is a mirror of our inner thoughts and beliefs. The body is always talking to us, if we will only take time to listen," she says.

To gain an understanding of the messages your body is sending you, it is important to think about the different functions of your body's organs and limbs.

As is experienced by the entity, there are dreams and visions and experiences. When only dreams, these *too*, are significant—but rather of that of the physical health, or physical conditions. In visions there is oft the *interbetween* giving expressions that make for an awakening between the mental consciousness, or that that has been turned over and over in the physical consciousness and mind being weighed with that the self holds as its ideal. In visions where spiritual awakenings, these most often are seen in symbols or signs, to the entity; for, as the training of self's consciousness in a manner of interpreting the visions would be in expressions of eye, hand, mouth, posture, or the like, these are *interpreted* in thine own language. When these are, then, in symbols of such, know the awakening is at hand. (262-9)

Back: support, courage. Have you been stabbed in the back by someone? Do you feel unsupported?

Bladder: could indicate anger at someone or a situation; or a need to release and let go of some situation to the Divine.

Blood: life force; strength; personal ideas and ideals (from 900-271)

Breast: is a symbol of nurturing and motherly love. Do you need nurturing? Or perhaps you're nurturing someone or some situation too much.

Ears: is there something you don't want to hear? Hay says that earaches affect children who "have to listen to stuff going on in the household they really don't want to hear." Perhaps there's something you should be listening to.

Eyes: outlook or vision (900-285); all-seeing (137-45). If you're having eye trouble, it could mean you're not willing to look at something occurring in your life.

Feet: pathway (900-37); represent our under-"stand"-ing. Is there some problem or issue you need to reflect upon? Are you putting your best foot forward?

Hands: how are you handling things? Are you handling too much? Or do you have a grip on a situation?

Hair: reasoning process; knots in hair indicate kinks in reasoning process (137-41); gray hair—wisdom or knowledge (900-156)

Head: attitude, orientation, or approach (294-131); headless—losing the head in duty (137-36). Are you getting ahead? Are you letting things go to your head?

Heart: love, energy, enthusiasm; heart problems could indicate a lack of love, not only from others but of love of self.

Knees: flexibility, ability to bend; also bowing to divine will (472-1)

Legs: foundation; principles, stepping forward. If we have difficulties here it could mean we have a reluctance to move with the flow of life.

Lungs: breath; need for more oxygen (440-2). If we're having difficulty with our lungs, we could feel smothered by a life experience or perhaps not worthy of taking up space on this planet. Matthew Fox, former Catholic priest who was silenced by the Vatican and author of *Creation Spirituality,* says that our breathing connects us with the Divine.

Neck: There's probably nothing more annoying than a stiff neck. This condition affects even our simplest movements. A stiff neck represents our inability to be flexible in our thoughts.

Skin: Are you thick-skinned and don't let too many things bother you? Or are you thin-skinned? Do you let things get under your skin too easily?

Stomach: the center of our digestive process. Is there something you're having difficulty "stomaching," or an issue, perhaps a change in your life, that you're not "digesting" or assimilating.

Teeth: spoken words (136-49); false teeth—sharp words (136-7); gold teeth—spiritual truths (288-14)

Throat: personal will; creativity; communication. Are you having difficulty expressing your creativity or speaking up?

THE UNIVERSE SPEAKS
THROUGH YOUR ENVIRONMENT

The conditions of our homes, cars, and offices are often an indication of how balanced or unbalanced we are in body, mind, and spirit. Even the Earth's ever-increasing natural upheavals and climatic changes are indications of the unhealthy and unbalanced conditions of our lives.

Violet Shelley suggests in *Symbols and the Self* that "If we want to know what is going on within ourselves, we need only to look at what is going on outside ourselves. The Cayce readings went so far as to suggest that if we want to know how we stand with our God, we need only to look at how we stand with our brother."

THE BODY/AUTOMOBILE CONNECTION

Very often in our dreams, as well as in our waking lives, our automobiles provide symbolic messages to us about our bodies.

In *Dreams—Your Magic Mirror*, Elsie Sechrist writes, "An automobile often symbolizes the physical body, because the body is the mechanical vehicle—'the means of transport'—of the eternal you, the soul. Therefore, in a dream, the driving mechanism of a car can represent the various anatomical parts of the dreamer."

This can also be true for waking visions or realizations.

Every time Jane entered her car, she groaned at the sight of the litter strewn about. Papers were on the floor. There were a few soda cans tucked under the seat, and sand and mud were embedded in the carpet.

At the same time, she was hearing people around her mentioning the Cayce apple diet. Then one day, while she was unlocking the door to the car, she realized that her car along with the overheard conversations were messages telling her that she needed to cleanse her body and go on the apple diet. With her commitment made to adhering to the diet, she also cleaned her car, which she believed symbolized her willingness to purify her system.

Another woman mentioned that her car wouldn't start, yet her garage mechanic could not find anything wrong with it. After giving it some thought, she realized that her travel schedule over the previous few weeks had left her weary, and she just needed to stay home and rest.

Gas gauges are also a good indicator of how well you're paying attention to yourself. If you continually let your car run on empty, you may need to refuel your body either nutritionally or with rest, and perhaps spiritually as well.

SYMBOLS AND YOUR HOME

In the establishing of the home, make it as that which may be the pattern of the heavenly home. . . Make thine home, thine abode, where an angel would desire to visit, where an angel would seek to be a guest. (480-20)

If your physical environment is in a state of disarray, this could mean it's time to pay more attention to the needs of your body, your mind, or your spirit.

Clutter could indicate that you need to do some serious cleaning and purging. It may be a time for a fast, or it may be time to eliminate some unnecessary activities which may be robbing your energy.

Clogged plumbing is usually an indication of emotions that are not flowing freely. Even the electrical system in your house might send messages to you about the state of the life force in your body.

In *The Secret Language of Signs*, Denise Linn writes,

"When a person begins a spiritual quest, his or her personal electrical field often will go through a change. This can affect the surrounding electrical fields."

This can not only occur at the beginning of a spiritual quest, but also at various stages of spiritual growth when your vibration rate rises.

Cayce said our homes represent our mental conditions, as stated in the following reading:

> In this, we find the houses, homes, places, representing the abode, the indwelling of the individuals as are seen in the dream. The actions representing those mental conditions as come to each of the individuals seen in dream . . . (900-53)

The various rooms in a house also have different meanings. In *The Encyclopedia of Symbolism*, Kevin Todeschi says that the basement may be associated with sexuality; the attic, to our higher consciousness; a closet may indicate something hidden; and a hallway symbolizes a passageway or journey.

The rooms in our homes also have different meanings:

Attic: high ideals, upper levels of consciousness; stored memories

Basement: root of the problem; sexuality; subconscious forces (140-8)

Bathroom: elimination, purification; need for attunement (140-18)

Bedroom: intimate relationships; sexuality; need for rest

Closet: inner self; air of mystery or misunderstanding (900-359). Is there something you're hiding—"skeletons"? Or perhaps something you're ready to reveal—"coming out of the closet."

Dining room: nourishment—physical, mental, or spiritual; digestion and assimilation (900-170); fullness (900-152)

Door: an opportunity; could signify a new phase of your life; slamming door—closing many of the avenues of expression (137-109)

Floor: foundation or support; has something floored you?

Hall: transition; passage

Kitchen: nourishment or creativity. What are you cooking up?

Laundry: Are things piling up? Do you have to clean up your act? Or are you spilling too many sordid details of your life?

Living room: daily activities

Porch: outside of self; insecurity

Roof: pinnacle of thought or understanding (900-105); protection; security; shelter

Stairs: a new level of consciousness; may be a warning to watch your step or take one step at a time

Wall: obstacle

Window: vision; awareness

For the symbols, signs, omens, all have been and are a part of the experience of the entity—and have at times been a manifested interest . . . As has been indicated, much might be said as to the symbols and those influences—but apply that which has been indicated, looking within self more and more; and we will find more peace, more harmony, more understanding. (2029-1)

Your decorating tastes may also symbolically represent your past lives. "When we take the time to look at these choices objectively, we can learn a lot about ourselves and where we have been," says Violet Shelley.

Decorating with Shaker furniture may indicate that you had a incarnation in that religious sect. A Southwest motif could suggest a Native American past life. Oak furniture and lace doilies patterned after that which was in vogue at the turn of the century might indicate a Victorian-period incarnation.

THE SYMBOLIC RELATIONSHIP OF THE BODY AND THE REVELATION

And in The Revelation study as this: Know, as there is given each emblem, each condition, it is representing or presenting to self a study of thine own body, with all of its emotions, all of its faculties. All of its physical centers represent experiences through which thine own mental and spiritual and physical being pass. For it is indeed the revelation of self. (1173-8)

Archetypal symbology and references to the body can be found in studying The Revelation. We can become more aligned with our spiritual purposes and receptive to a higher power that can flow through our chakras by reciting the Lord's Prayer, while visualizing these centers, perhaps along with their corresponding colors.

Begin at the pituitary, the seventh chakra, located in the center of the forehead. This is referred to as the master gland and commonly thought of as the seat of the third eye. Visualize the color white or violet.
Our Father which art in heaven

Move to the pineal, or the crown or sixth chakra, visualizing gold or indigo.
Hallowed be Thy name

Move now to the fifth chakra, the thyroid center, visualizing silver or blue.
Thy kingdom come, Thy will be done

Then referring to the four lower centers collectively:
In earth

Moving our attention to the three upper centers collectively:
As it is in heaven

Focus now on the root or first chakra, where the gonads are located, visualizing red.
Give us this day our daily bread

Now to the solar plexus, third chakra, or the adrenal center. Visualize yellow.
And forgive us our debts as we forgive our debtors

Visualize orange while placing your awareness on your second chakra, the cells of Leydig center.

And lead us not into temptation

Moving to the heart center, the seat of the thymus, visualize green.
But deliver us from evil

Back to the fifth chakra, the thyroid, visualize blue.
For Thine is the kingdom

Return to the pineal, visualizing indigo.
And the power

While visualizing violet, finish with:
And the glory forever.
Amen.

Chapter 8

SYMBOLS IN ACTION:
RITUAL AND RITES OF PASSAGE

Ritual and rites of passage were used by ancient and indigenous cultures to honor major life transitions. These ceremonies were used to help the individual or individuals integrate the new life experience into their being. These rites were performed with sincerity and intention; not merely by going through the motions. They symbolize the connection of humankind with the Divine. Cayce summed it up in the following reading:

We realize it is the spirit and not the letter of the law that is so important and the ritual is a symbol and not an activity—rarely at all. (2072-10)

"Rituals are physical enactments of spiritual journeys," says David Fontana, author of *The Dream Ency-clopedia*. "They can symbolize progression toward enlightenment . . . or the journey of death and subsequent rebirth, in which we sacrifice our identity and pass renewed into the next stage of life."

Many counselors, psychologists, and anthropologists feel that life transitions should be marked by "rites of passage. This term was first used by Charles-Arnold van Gennep, an anthropologist in the late 1920s. At that time, he identified seven major life events that need to be ritualized in order to honor the passing from one phase of life to another.

In addition to birth, marriage, and death, he stressed the importance of honoring times of entry, initiation, demonstration, and attainment. Entry refers to a time when we make new contact through friendships, career moves, or perhaps moving to a neighborhood. He referred to initiation as the occasions when we open ourselves up to higher levels of consciousness and the trials associated with walking our talk.

Gennep says we must bring a sense of sacredness to those times when we share our experiences and knowledge with others, through teaching, healing, even writing, which he referred to as demonstration. This can be done by a moment of silence either alone or in the presence of others. Barbara Dossey, co-author of *Rituals of Healing*, finds it helpful to light a candle before she begins writing. The light helps her focus.

We also need to honor our accomplishments and those times when we feel fulfilled. Graduation ceremonies are prime examples of honoring life events whether it be from kindergarten, grade school, high school, or college. Other goals that we have attained can also be honored through ritual. Finishing a book can be celebrated by buying yourself a gift or by taking a long walk on the beach or in the woods.

"The purpose of ritual is to increase balance and connection within ourselves, with each other, with the world, and with the subtle but powerful rhythms and energies of the cosmos and the spiritual realm," say Renee Beck and Sydney Barbara Metrick, authors of *The Art of Ritual: A Guide to Creating and Performing Your Own Rituals for Growth and Change.*

We are perhaps more familiar with ritual in religions, which allow us to connect with sacred power. In the Roman Catholic church, seven Christian sacraments, thought to be set forth by Christ, are honored. Varying only slightly from those that van Gennep identified, these include baptism, communion, confirmation, marriage, confession, ordination, or extreme unction (now known as the sacrament of the sick). Of these, confession and extreme unction are not recognized within other Christian denominations.

"A sacrament is a sacred sign of worship by which we come into intimate personal contact with Christ and receive His grace," says Anthony Wilhelm, author of *Christ Among Us: A Modern Presentation of the Catholic Faith.* "By these meetings with Christ we are joined most intimately with the whole Trinity. It is the Spirit within us that unites us with Christ in the sacraments, and they join us ultimately with the Father."

Baptism affirms a family's responsibility toward rearing a child with spiritual principles. As an adult, baptism signifies spiritual conversion or rebirth. Purification rites, such as bathing in a moving stream, are used in many tribal cultures for the purpose cleansing a polluted body, one that has been in contact with death or disease.

In *communion,* the *bread* represents the body of Christ, and the *wine* the blood of Christ. The *chalice,* according to Jung, symbolizes the spiritual womb. In *Transformation Symbolism in the Mass,* referring to the Catholic mass, he says, "The lifting up of the chalice in the air prepares the spiritualization . . . of the wine. This is confirmed by the invocation to the Holy Ghost that immediately follows . . . The invocation serves to infuse the wine with holy spirit, for it is the Holy Ghost who begets, fulfills, and transforms." He further explains that the act of placing the chalice on the right side of the Host symbolizes the blood flowing from the right side of Christ.

In the following reading, Cayce describes the symbolism of the ritual of communion:

And then those periods of taking leave after the establishing of the emblems as His body and blood, as a ritual for those who would honor and bring to remembrance those experiences through which each soul passes in putting on the whole armor of the Christ. (5749-10)

Marriage represents the commitment and responsibility we have toward our partner. It also symbolizes the merger of heaven and earth, of God's love finding expression between two people. The ceremony honors the commitment of two people to form a sacred union, which as a whole far surpasses what the two represent individually. The wedding dress, the ring, and in some cultures tattoos represent the new social status of the two joined in this ceremony.

Extreme unction, or last rites, allows the dying to release their spirit into the afterlife, bringing closure in this life.

However, today the *sacrament of the sick* is administered for those seeking healing of body, mind, or spirit.

Many cultures and religions have elaborate funerary rites which mark the passage of the soul of the deceased into the afterlife. Ancient Egyptians buried the mummified remains of the deceased along with food and other essentials. These offerings were thought to sustain the person in the afterlife.

Indigenous tribes also have rites of passage for boys moving into adulthood. These rites could include periods of fasting, tests of strength and endurance, as well as circumcision, which is found in modern Judaic practices as well. Girls are also subjected to fertility rites on the onset of menstruation to mark their passage into womanhood.

"Since rituals make use of the same stuff that dreams are made of—symbolism, fantasy, myths, and metaphors—they address themselves to the most primitive and profound level of experience," says Onno van der Hart, in *Rituals in Psychotherapy*.

Daily Rituals

"The function of ritual, as I understand it, is to give form to the human life, not in the way of a mere surface arrangement, but in depth," says Joseph Campbell in *Myths to Live By*. And the depth of ritual can also be brought into our daily lives. It needn't be reserved for major life transitions.

Prayer can either be an act of going through the motions or a sacred moment honoring our connection with the Creator. Position of the hands and the body signify our submission to divine will.

The following is a reading in which Cayce refers to both meditation and prayer:

> For the entity indeed is the temple of the living God, or the Creative Forces, and *there* the self may meet not only its own self but its Maker in meditation, in prayer, as well as in choice of the application of its ideal in its relationship to others. (1782-1)

Meditation can be merely an act of quieting the mind,

of unwinding from the day's pressures, or it can be a time honoring our alignment with our Creator's will.

There are many instances in the readings in which Cayce set forth a variety of methods for preparing for meditation. These preparations or rituals set the stage for this period of quietness where we remove ourselves from our daily concerns. If you walk into the main conference room at A.R.E. headquarters at noontime, you can see many of these rituals being used by staff and visitors as they begin their period of meditation. These include head and neck exercises as well as the alternate nostril breathing exercises. If done mindfully, these acts signal the body and the emotions that it is time to put the morning's cares aside.

In the following reading, Cayce describes the use of incense and toning in preparation for meditation:

> For this body—not for everybody—odors would have much to do with the ability of the entity to meditate . . . Begin with that which is Oriental in its nature—Oriental incense. Let the mind become, as it were, attuned to such by the humming, producing those sounds of o-o-o—ah-ah-ah-umm-o-o-o; not as to become monotonous, but "feel" the essence of the incense through the body-forces in its motion of body. This will open the kundalini forces of the body. Then direct same to be a blessing to others. These arise from the creative center of the body itself, and as they go through the various centers direct same; else they may become greater disturbing than helpful. Surround self ever with that purpose, "not my will, O God, but Thine be done, ever," and the entity will gain vision, perception, and—most of all—judgment. (2823-3)

In addition to the head and neck exercises, the breathing exercises, and the chanting, one Virginia Beach study group includes the use of incense to purify the participants and the room as preparation for meditation. This ritual creates within it a signal or an emotional response that makes the time more meaningful and representative of the group's willingness to be of one mind and one purpose during the following twenty minutes of connection with the Divine.

According to Meredith Puryear, prayer services coordinator for A.R.E, Cayce said that incense, particularly violet or myrrh, awakens or quickens the spiritual body. He, however, in at least one instance warned against sandalwood because it entraps the soul in the lower chakras.

Establishing our own rituals prior to meditation is also helpful. It sets the stage and allows our consciousness to prepare for that quiet time with our Creator, as emphasized in the following reading:

> In whatever manner that thine own consciousness is a cleansing of the body and of the mind, that ye may present thyself *clean* before thyself and before thy God, *do!* Whether washing of the body with water, purging of the same with oils, or surrounding same with music or incense. But *do that thy consciousness directs* thee! Not questioning! For he that doubteth has already built his barrier! (826-11)

Preparing a meal, if done with mindfulness, can signify our willingness to care for our bodies, as temples of God. *Bathing* can symbolize a washing away of the day's worries or other negative emotions.

Gina uses the bath to rejuvenate her soul and her body after particularly stressful times. She lights candles and incense, puts on healing music, and pours essential oils into the water. Her actions are thoughtful and performed slowly. She doesn't rush around turning on the cassette player or lighting the candles. She intentionally slows her pace, which begins to create the sacred environment to allow peace and tranquillity to ease away tension and anxiety. As she soaks in the hot water, she prays for healing and visualizes herself being calm and divinely protected. Even the act of letting the water flow down the drain symbolizes her cares being washed away.

The entity then finds an interest in the activities of all characters of *ritual;* not as to what it *does* but the *why* of same in the experience—the emotions created by same. (1473-1)

RITUALS FOR SPECIAL MOMENTS

We are all familiar with rituals associated with holidays. At Christmas we decorate the evergreen tree, which symbolizes the winter solstice and the coming of the new year. At Easter, we hunt for eggs, with eggs symbolizing the new beginning, the rebirth. Setting off fireworks on the Fourth of July symbolizes the bombs bursting in air and the effort it took for the United States to become a sovereign nation. Halloween provides us with a time to connect with our community and also with the opportunity to dress up and be playful. And at Thanksgiving, gathering together for a festive meal provides us with the moment to give thanks for all our blessings. These celebrations, along with other cyclical events such as birthdays and anniversaries, are opportunities for us to honor the very essence of our lives.

Each year on his birthday, David takes a walk in the woods. He packs a lunch and his journal and writes down his accomplishments for the past year and his goals for the following year. In his pack is also a thermos of hot chocolate. When he was a child, he and his father would often go off into the woods on his birthday and celebrate by toasting with hot chocolate. His father would tell him how proud he was of how much he'd grown and give him encouragement for the upcoming year.

By putting our consciousness into our celebrations, we give depth to our lives. And this needn't be limited to holiday celebrations. Other events or acts in our lives can also be given new meaning by our being mindful and observant. In the following reading, Cayce reminds us that it is our intentions which affect our experiences:

It is the spirit with which ye do a thing, the purpose that brings weal or woe in its effect in the experience. (3285-2)

Writing a letter to an old friend can be a sacred act of honoring the friendship. After leaving her marriage, Claire kept her distance from three friends she had made through her ex-husband's business associates. While their friendships were very meaningful to her, she needed the space to regroup and form her own identity before reconnecting with these women. On the eve of the six-month anniversary of the end of her marriage, she sat at her computer and wrote a letter to each, letting her heart guide the way to find the words to share with each one. She put on soft music, lit a few candles, and said a silent prayer that the right words be found to express her feelings clearly and without malice toward her ex-husband. To Claire this symbolized the willingness to take a risk, to stand up for her decision to leave the marriage, and also to no longer let her ex-husband's anger keep her from being herself and keep her from the people she loved.

In those things, then, *innate* and partially manifesting themselves in the experience of the entity, those things that have to do with mystery or ritual, while of interest often, and hold for the entity something of an attraction, should not be often indulged in, unless there be much more of reason than of speculative interests. (1234-1)

EXERCISE:

Take a moment to think of a simple daily activity that you can make more meaningful by bringing some symbolic gesture into the event.

Some suggestions:

• Say a blessing at the beginning of a meal.

• Stand in front of an east-facing window upon arising and give thanks for the new day.

• Hug your children or your partner before they leave the house for the day.

And to make the next major holiday more meaningful, begin now to think of ways to bring symbolic gestures of honoring the moment into the event. For example:

• For Easter, buy a purple tablecloth to represent the resurrection of Christ.

• Plant a garden, or a single flower plant, to celebrate the beginning of spring.

• Plan a special birthday celebration for someone special in your life.

• Be sure to include some personal symbols in your holiday rituals.

Conclusion

And in whatever environ, whether in body or out of the body, the consciousness or awareness of the experiences as in relationship to Creative Forces makes for that which draws the entity nearer to its oneness with its source or else through his own self it separates self. For as has been given, there is nothing in heaven, in earth, that may separate a soul from its Maker but the entity itself.

In given then these signs, these omens for the entity, for this entity it will be found that there are days—as in astrological, as in numerological experience; there are flowers, there are jewels, there are those things in its experience that add to the *influences* in and about the entity. And how much the *entity* accredits or *gives* the force of power *to* those influences depends upon how much they come to mean in the experience of the entity . . .

Insofar as the entity allows itself to be influenced by same, they have the influence upon the entity. (1183-1)

Gaining an understanding of the symbols that we draw into our awareness is essential for our continued spiritual development and for a deeper understanding of ourselves. Symbols remind us to pause, take a break from the treadmill of life, and to look within. The appearance of signs, either outwardly or in our dreams, is a signal for us to shift our focus to who we are—our beingness—rather what we do and what we accomplish.

"Symbols help us to shift our own focus from the world of outer things and reveal to us the real Self within," says Shelley.

Carolyn Gelone, a past-life regressionist and fung shui expert, says that signs don't always appear to help us make decisions. "Because our Creator gave us free will,

these symbols often don't appear until after we've chosen a direction or taken some action," she says. "These
signs can be either affirming our decision, or they may
let us know that we need to rethink our decisions."

Whether the symbols attempting to wake us from our
daily lives are interpreted literally, symbolically, or even
metaphorically, they are important to spend time reflecting upon. Jung said there are not only symbolic
dreams, but there are symbolic acts and situations as
well. For instance, when I get an urge to clean out the
closets in my home, I know that it's a clue that subcon-
sciously I'm working on some issue. I'm purging my subconscious of some consciousness that I need to integrate
into my life.

Edgar Cayce said the best service we can provide others is to share what we have learned from our experience. The process of writing this book reminded me of
birthing my children. It began with the gestation of an
idea, the promise of a healthy pregnancy or period of
writing, and with it an excitement of awaiting the new
creation. Then there were some minor complications,
which caused some concern.

In the last couple of weeks of writing and revising, I
went through periods of wishing the project were over,
just as I had in the final month of pregnancy for both of
my children. Then I prepared to spend the last few days
at home, away from the office, for the actual birth of the
book. I "nested" around my office, tidying up a few last-
minute details for other projects before leaving. And
then I did the same in my home. I putzed around, pick-
ing up three-day-old newspapers, doing a little laundry,
and washing the dishes—a little ritual I usually perform
anytime I need to focus for long periods of time on my
writing.

Then labor began, and with it arrived the final day of
reading all of the words that had joined together over the

last few months to make one whole creation, much like the cells of the body would form a child. I'd sit at the computer for long hours, then occasionally rise from my chair to pace around the room, take a walk, reflect on a particularly tough idea or sentence that I felt wasn't clear enough. I remember pacing many times as well during the labor of my children, during stronger contractions.

The first few chapters went rather smoothly. Then as the hours ticked by and I grew weary from staring at the computer screen, I became irritable and impatient. I knew the end was in sight when I began to cuss at my dog who tripped me up every time I moved from my desk to retrieve some more coffee or a handful of nuts or dried fruit. It was symbolic of my saying a few choice words to my doctor as she examined me in the final stages of the birth of my son. I was in transition; birth was imminent.

Then when the final page was printed, I sat back, took a deep breath, and breathed a sigh of relief as I looked proudly at the stack of bright white paper with those words of creation printed upon them. I even cried a few tears of relief and joy, just as I had with my children. An event worth celebrating.

> The soul is the real self, the continuous self. The mind is the builder, continuous to the extent that it is constructive . . . and that which is constructive and good is continuous. (1620-1)

The symbols that are important to us are carried with us from lifetime to lifetime. We are constantly building our personal symbols dictionary.

"There is much material in the Edgar Cayce life readings that indicates that we ourselves are symbols of everything we have built by our thinking and actions in this life and in previous lives," writes Violet Shelley. "In order to know our real Self, therefore, we need to start examining the patterns we create and the relationships and problems that we draw to us. We can then interpret what is happening in our conscious lives in much the same way as we interpret what lies at the unconscious level, remembering 'As without, so within.'"

While it's important to learn from the symbols of our pasts, we must also be conscious of the symbols we create for our future. Singer/songwriter Tracy Chapman states it eloquently in her song *New Beginning*. She reminds us that as the new millennium approaches, we need to create new symbols and new signs—a new language of the soul—for our new world, one in which Cayce says brings the promise of a thousand years of peace.

May you enjoy discovering the guiding lights along your journey of life.

◆ ◆ ◆

Objects and Their Frequencies in Dreams: The Hall/Van de Castle Research Findings

Dream psychologists have been fascinated with the question of frequency for particular symbols. For example, when someone dreams of a crocodile twice in one week, is that out of the ordinary? The best study ever conducted to analyze the symbols content of dreams was done by Drs. Calvin Hall and Robert Van de Castle. It documents the frequency of nearly 1,200 symbols in the dreams of 1,000 college students, with data analyzed separately for men and women.

Dr. Van de Castle and the family of Dr. Hall have given A.R.E. Press permission to reprint this valuable research resource. Readers may find it useful in assessing when a particular symbol is occurring more often than might be expected.

As comprehensive as this research study is, there are still some limitations that should be kept in mind. The data was collected more than twenty-five years ago, so something that we consider as everyday as a personal computer doesn't appear in the data tables. Also these were the dreams of young adults which may have some effect on dream symbology. When the same type of object was referred to by different names, the frequencies were combined under one name. For example, car, automobile, and Ford were included under "automobile." Few such combinations were made, however, because the compilers wanted to preserve the specificity of objects in these norms; they did not include "taxi cab" or "bus" under "automobile" but gave each of them a separate heading. Cross references are made to objects that were combined. No object was entered under more than one heading.

There are three capitalized objects in the list. These are Country, State, and University, and in each instance they include all references to a specific Country, e.g., England; a specific State, e.g., Michigan; or a specific University, e.g., Western Reserve University.

Appendix A
Incidence of Objects in 500 Male and 500 Female Dreams

M. = Male   F. = Female   B. = Both

	M.	F.	B.		M.	F.	B.
abdomen		2	2	attic	1	2	3
abutment	1		1	attire	2		2
accelerator, car	3	1	4	auditorium	4	5	9
accordion	1		1	automobile	86	63	149
adrenaline	1		1	avenue (see street)			
advertisement	1	1	2				
aerial	1		1	back, body	4	4	8
afterbirth		1	1	back, chair	1		1
aircraft carrier	2		2	back, couch	1		1
airfield	1		1	backstage (see stage)			
airplane	16	8	24	back yard (see yard)			
aisle	4	6	10	bacon		1	1
album, record		1	1	bag	3	2	5
alcohol		1	1	bag, golf	1		1
alfalfa		1	1	bag, mail	1		1
alley	1	2	3	baggage		3	3
altar	2	3	5	bait	2		2
ambulance	2	1	3	bakery		1	1
ammunition	2		2	balcony	1	2	3
anastomosis	1		1	ball, any type	11	2	13
anatomy		1	1	ballfield		1	1
animal	10	8	18	balloon	1	1	2
ankle		2	2	bandages	1	2	3
anklets		1	1	bank, building		2	2
antiques		1	1	bank, river	4	1	5
apartment	6	10	16	bankbook		1	1
ape	1		1	bar, ballet		2	2
aperture	1		1	bar, tavern	6	4	10
apparatus		1	1	barn	5	2	7
appendix	1		1	barracks, army	4		4
apple		2	2	barrel, container	1		1
arches	1		1	base, baseball	2		2
archway		1	1	basement	7	3	10
area	6		6	basket	1	2	3
arena	1		1	bassinet		1	1
arm	24	20	44	bat, baseball		1	1
armholes	1		1	bathtub		5	5
armor	1		1	battlefield	3		3
arrows	1		1	battleship	1		1
arsenic	1		1	bay	3		3
artillery, weapons	1		1	bayonet		1	1
ashtray	1		1	beach	6	5	11

	M.	F.	B.		M.	F.	B.
beads		1	1	bouquet, flower		1	1
beak	1		1	bowl	1	1	2
beams	1		1	bowling alley		2	2
bear, animal	3	1	4	box	5	8	13
beard	1		1	box, music	1		1
bed	21	20	41	bra		1	1
bedspread	1	1	2	bracelet		3	3
beer	4	3	7	brains	1		1
bell	4	8	12	brakes, car	3	2	5
bellows	1		1	branch, tree	1		1
belly		1	1	bread		1	1
belongings	1	1	2	breakwater		1	1
belts		1	1	breasts	4	1	5
bench		3	3	breath	2	1	3
bible		1	1	brick	1	2	3
bicycle	9	8	17	bridge	12	7	19
billboard		1	1	bristle, brush	1		1
billfold		2	2	brooches		1	1
bills, money	5	1	6	brook	1	1	2
bills, store		1	1	broom	1		1
binoculars		1	1	brush	2		2
birds	4	1	5	bugs		2	2
blackboard	2	1	3	building	27	36	63
blackheads		1	1	bullets	4	2	6
blankets	3	1	4	bulletin	1		1
bleachers		2	2	bump		2	2
blimp	1		1	bumper	1		1
blinds, venetian	1	1	2	bunks	2		2
blisters, body		1	1	buoy		1	1
block, city	2	5	7	bus	6	14	20
blood	6	5	11	butter		1	1
blouse	1	1	2	button	3		3
boar	1		1	button, firing	1		1
board	3	1	4				
boat	10	12	22	cabana		1	1
body, human or animal	18	6	24	cabbage		1	1
bolt, hardware	2		2	cabin	5	2	7
bomb, explosive	4	6	10	cabinet	1	1	2
bond, security		1	1	cable	1		1
bone, collar		1	1	cafeteria	5	4	9
bone, hip		1	1	cage	2		2
bone, jaw		1	1	cake	3	2	5
bonfire		1	1	calf, animal		1	1
book	10	7	17	camellia		1	1
bookcase		1	1	camera	1		1
booth, restaurant	3	1	4	camp	1	3	4
boots	3	2	5	campus	7	4	11
bottle	2	3	5	can	1		1
boulder	2		2	canal	1	3	4
				cancer		3	3

	M.	F.	B.		M.	F.	B.
candles	1		1	clothes	15	21	36
candy	3	2	5	clouds	5	1	6
canoe	4	1	5	club, country	4		4
canyon		1	1	coal	2	1	3
cap, head gear	1	1	2	coat	9	15	24
capsules		1	1	cockpit	1		1
car (see automobile)				cockroaches		1	1
cardboard	1		1	cocktail	1		1
carburetor	2		2	coffee	3	1	4
card, AGO	1		1	coin (see money)			
card, calling	1		1	coke		2	2
card, Christmas	2		2	collar	1	1	2
card, class		1	1	college	5	11	16
cards, playing	4	5	9	cologne		3	3
carnations		1	1	compartment, house	1	1	2
carnival	1		1	condom	1		1
carpet	1	3	4	containers	1		1
carriage	1		1	contraption	1	2	3
cart		4	4	contrivance	1		1
cartoon		1	1	controls, airplane	1	1	2
cases, container		3	3	convertible (see automobile)			
cash register	1		1	cookies	1	1	2
castle	2		2	cooler, boston	1		1
cat	2	7	9	co-op, store	2		2
cattails		1	1	cooper		1	1
cave	5	1	6	cord	1	1	2
cavity, tooth	1		1	corner, street	14	13	27
ceiling	3	2	5	corral	1		1
cellar	2	2	4	corridor	2	6	8
cement	1	1	2	corset		1	1
cemetery	2	1	3	costume	3	8	11
chair	10	17	27	cot	1	1	2
champagne	1		1	cottage		1	1
chandeliers		1	1	cotton	1	1	2
chapel		1	1	couch	2	4	6
chart	1		1	counter	7	5	12
cheek		3	3	Country (specific)	25	5	30
cheese	1		1	country	11	9	20
chest, body	2	2	4	coupe (see automobile)			
chickens	1		1	court, basketball	1		1
church	6	11	17	court, tennis		1	1
chute	1		1	cover, slide rule	1		1
cigarette	1	1	2	cows	1		1
city	64	64	128	crack	1	1	2
clearing	1		1	crackers	2		2
cliff	7	5	12	cradle		1	1
clock	1	1	2	cream	1		1
closet	2	9	11	creek	1		1
clot	1		1	crevasse	1		1
cloth	1	1	2	crocodiles	1		1

	M.	F.	B.
cross, red	1		1
cross, religious		1	1
crossing, railroad	1	1	2
crow		1	1
crown	2		2
cruiser, police (see automobile)			
cup	1	1	2
cupboards		3	3
cupcake	1		1
curb	1	3	4
curls		1	1
currency (see money)			
curtain	2	2	4
cut	3	1	4
cutlass	1		1
dam	1		1
dance hall	1	1	2
darts	1	1	2
davenport	1		1
deck, boat	3		3
decorations		3	3
deer	3		3
den, room	1	1	2
depressor, tongue		1	1
desert	1		1
desk	8	13	21
destroyer	1		1
diagram	1		1
diamonds	1	3	4
diapers		2	2
diner		1	1
dining hall		1	1
dinosaur		1	1
diploma		1	1
dirt	2	1	3
dish	1	3	4
display	2	2	4
district	1	2	3
ditch		1	1
divan		1	1
diving board		2	2
dock		1	1
dog	9	10	19
doll	1	2	3
dollars (see money)			
donkey		1	1
door	46	57	103
doorbell (see bell)			
doorknob		1	1

	M.	F.	B.
doorway	2	2	4
dope		1	1
dormitory	4	42	46
doughnut	3		3
downspout	1		1
downstairs	13	10	23
downtown	7	9	16
drain, water	1	1	2
drapes	2		2
drawer	2	7	9
drawstring	1		1
dress	8	31	39
dresser		5	5
drink	6	5	11
driveway	6	4	10
drug	1		1
duck	2	1	3
dummy	1	1	2
dungarees		1	1
dynamos	1		1
earrings		2	2
ears	2	1	3
earth	1	1	2
eaves	1		1
egg		2	2
elbow	1	1	2
elephants	2		2
elevator	5	8	13
embankment		1	1
emeralds		1	1
engine	3	1	4
engine, fire	1	1	2
entrails		1	1
entrance	3	4	7
envelope	1	1	2
equipment	3	2	5
equipment, fire	1		1
eraser		1	1
escalator		2	2
escape, fire	1	2	3
excavations	1		1
extinguisher, fire	1		1
eyebrows		1	1
eyelashes	1	1	2
eyelid	1		1
eyes	8	16	24
façade	1		1
face	14	32	46

	M.	F.	B.		M.	F.	B.
factory		1	1	fur	1	3	4
fair	2		2	furnace	2		2
fare		1	1	furnishings	1	2	3
farm	3	1	4	furniture	1	3	4
feathers	1		1	furrows		1	1
features, facial	1		1	fuselage	1		1
feelers		1	1				
feet	5	6	11	gangplank		1	1
fence	4	3	7	garage	5	2	7
fender	3		3	garden		2	2
field	15	4	19	garden, beer	1		1
figurine	1	1	2	garnets		1	1
file, box		1	1	gas, anesthetic	2		2
film	1		1	gas, tear	1		1
finger	3	4	7	gasoline	6	1	7
fingerprints	1		1	gate	1		1
fingertip	1		1	gear, belongings	1		1
fire	7		7	gear, landing	2		2
firecrackers	1		1	genital	3		3
fireplace	1		1	gift		4	4
fish	5	3	8	giraffes	1		1
flames	2	2	4	girders	1		1
flamethrower	1		1	glass, container	2	1	3
flashlight	1		1	glass, window	3		3
flask		1	1	glasses, eye	2	7	9
fleas	1		1	gloves	2	1	3
float, homecoming		1	1	gold	2	3	5
flood	1	1	2	golf club	3		3
floor	29	30	59	gondola	1		1
flooring	1		1	goods, material	1		1
flower	2	8	10	gown	1	7	8
flowerpot	1		1	grain	1		1
fluid	1		1	grass	2	5	7
foliage	1	1	2	grave		1	1
food	7	5	12	graveyard		1	1
foot	2	3	5	grease	1		1
forearm	1		1	grill		1	1
forehead	2	1	3	ground	19	13	32
forest	8	8	16	guinea pig		1	1
fork		1	1	gully	1		1
formation	1	1	2	gum		1	1
forts		1	1	gums		1	1
foundation		1	1	gun	18	4	22
fountain	1	1	2	gym	7	1	8
fox	1	1	2				
foxhole		1	1	hail	1		1
frame, glasses		1	1	hair	8	24	32
frame, wooden	1		1	hall	10	20	30
frog		2	2	halter		1	1
fruit	1		1	ham	1		1

	M.	F.	B.		M.	F.	B.
hammer	1		1	ice cubes		1	1
hand	26	33	49	icing, cake	1		1
handbag	2	1	3	ink		2	2
handbook	1		1	insect		2	2
handcar	1		1	instruments	1		1
handle	2		2	intersection	1		
hanger, clothes	1		1	invitation, wedding		1	1
harbor	1	1	2	iron		1	1
hat	6	4	10	island	5		5
hawk	2		2				
head	17	19	36	jack, car	1		1
headlights	4		4	jacket	5	4	9
headquarters	1		1	jail	2		2
heart	4	3	7	jars		1	1
heels	2		2	jeans, blue		3	3
helicopter	2		2	jello		1	1
helmet	1		1	jelly		1	1
herd	1		1	jewelry		3	3
highway	12	1	13	jewels	1	1	2
hill	17	18	35	juice	1	1	2
hinges	1		1	jungle	2		2
hips	1	1	2	junk		2	2
hole	5	8	13				
home	47	71	118	kayak		1	1
hometown	3		3	kettle	1		1
hood, car	4		4	keys, door	4	2	6
hood, parka		1	1	keys, piano	1		1
horn	2		2	kidney		1	1
hornet		1	1	kit, tool	1		1
horse	4	5	9	kitchen	13	12	25
horse, water	1	1	2	kitten		3	3
hospital	4	13	17	kleenex	1	1	2
hotel	6	13	19	knees	2	4	6
house	83	77	160	knife	8	3	11
house, club	1		1	knitting		1	1
house, court		1	1				
house, export		1	1	laboratory		8	8
house, farm	1	1	2	lace		1	1
house, fraternity	10	1	11	lace, football	1		1
house, movie	3	1	4	ladder	4		4
housecoat		1	1	lake	9	18	27
hubcap	1		1	lambs		1	1
hull	1		1	lamps	1	2	3
hurricane	1		1	lance	1		1
hymn		2	2	land	1	3	4
				landmarks		1	1
ice	4		4	landscape	1	1	2
iceberg		1	1	lane		1	1
icebox	2		2	lap	4	1	5
ice cream	3		3	lapels		1	1

	M.	F.	B.		M.	F.	B.
launch		1	1	mansion	4		4
laundrateria		1	1	marble	2	1	3
lawn	2	4	6	marshland	2		2
lean-to	1		1	mascara		1	1
leather	1	1	2	mask		2	2
leaves		2	2	mats	1	2	3
ledge	4	1	5	mattress	1	1	2
legs	14	17	31	maze	1	1	2
legs, pant		1	1	meadow	1		1
lens		2	2	meat	1		1
leotards		1	1	medal	1		1
letter	5	7	12	medicine		2	2
lettuce		1	1	membrane		1	1
library	2	2	4	merchandise	1	1	2
license	2	1	3	mercury		1	1
lid		1	1	mezzanine		1	1
light	12	14	26	microphone	2		2
light, street	1		1	milk	2		2
light, traffic	1	1	2	mill	1		1
lighter, cigarette	1		1	mine		1	1
lighthouse		1	1	mint, money		1	1
lightning	3		3	mints, candy		1	1
limbs, legs or arms		2	2	mirror	2	4	6
limbs, tree	1		1	mist	2	1	3
linens		1	1	moccasins		1	1
lingerie		1	1	model, replica		1	1
linoleum		1	1	molding	1		1
lions	1		1	money	27	16	43
lips	1		1	monument		1	1
lipstick	1	2	3	moon		2	2
liquor	1	1	2	mop	1		1
liver		1	1	moss	1		1
lobby	2	3	5	motel		1	1
locker	3	2	5	motor	3	1	4
locomotives	1	2	3	motorboat	1		1
loft	1		1	motorcycle	1	2	3
log	1	2	3	mounds	1		1
lot	2	2	4	mountain	6		6
lot, parking	4	7	11	mouth	7	5	12
loud speaker		1	1	mouthpiece		1	1
lounge	2		2	movies	6	9	15
lumber	1		1	muck		1	1
lumps	1		1	mud	3	1	4
				mugs	1		1
machine	6	1	7	murals		1	1
machinery	2	1	3	muscles	1		1
magazine	2	4	6	mustache		1	1
mail	3	3	6				
mailbox	2		2	nails	3		3
mainland	1		1	napkin		2	2

	M.	F.	B.		M.	F.	B.
neck	4	6	10	pearls	1	1	2
necklace		2	2	peas	1	2	3
neckpiece	1		1	pebbles	1	1	2
needle	1	1	2	peepholes		1	1
negatives	1		1	pen		1	1
negligee	1	2	3	pencil		2	2
neighborhood	4	1	5	penis	2		2
nerve	1		1	perfume	1	1	2
nest	1		1	pew	1	1	2
newspaper	2	2	4	pheasant	1		1
nightclub	1	1	2	piano	3	4	7
nightgown	1	1	2	pickles	1		1
nipples	1		1	piccolo		1	1
nose	3	2	5	picture	8	7	15
notes	2	1	3	pie	1		1
nozzle		1	1	pier	3		3
				pig		1	1
ocean	4	5	9	pile	3	3	6
octopus		1	1	pill	1		1
office	8	9	17	pillar	1	1	2
oil	1		1	pillow	1	2	3
ointment	1		1	pimple		2	2
opening	1	2	3	pin	2	2	4
orchard	1		1	pin, bowling		1	1
orchid		2	2	pipe	3		3
organs, body	4	2	6	pistol	2	1	3
organs, sense		1	1	pit		2	2
orifice	1		1	plain	2		2
outfit, clothes	2	4	6	planet	1		1
overalls		1	1	planks		1	1
overcoats	1	1	2	plant, power	1		1
owl		1	1	plants	1		1
				plaster	1		1
package	3	5	8	plate, baseball	1		1
paddle		1	1	plate, charge		1	1
page	4	3	7	plate, license	2	1	3
paint	6	2	8	platform	9	2	11
painting		1	1	playground		1	1
pajamas	1	3	4	plumbing	1		1
pan		4	4	plums		1	1
panel	1	1	2	plywood	1		1
pants	14	16	30	pocket	10	2	12
paper	10	11	21	poker	1		1
park	5	5	10	pole	3		3
passageway	2	3	5	pole, fishing	1		1
passport		1	1	pole, telephone		1	1
patches	1		1	pond	1	4	5
path	5	3	8	pool	3	12	15
peaches		1	1	pool hall	1		1
peanut butter	1		1	popcorn		1	1

	M.	F.	B.		M.	F.	B.
porch	2	6	8	ring, napkin		1	1
port	2		2	river	7	8	15
possum		1	1	road	27	17	44
post		1	1	roadblock		1	1
post office	1	2	3	roast	1		1
pot		3	3	robe	3	1	4
potatoes	1	2	3	rock	3	3	6
powder	1	2	3	rocket	1		1
precipice	1		1	rod	1	2	3
pretzel		1	1	rod, fishing	1	1	2
print, foot	1		1	roof	4	6	10
prison	1	1	2	room	57	68	125
projection	1		1	room, back		4	4
puddle		2	2	room, ball	1	4	5
pulpit		1	1	room, basement		1	1
pump	2		2	room, bath	8	14	22
puppy	1	1	2	room, bed	12	16	28
purse		7	7	room, boiler	1	1	2
python	1		1	room, class	10	8	18
				room, dining	4	10	14
quail		1	1	room, dressing		3	3
quarters, rooms	2	1	3	room, front	2	1	3
				room, home	1		1
rabbit	1		1	room, hotel	2	2	4
rack	2	1	3	room, ironing		1	1
radio	5	2	7	room, living	10	18	28
rafters	1		1	room, locker	2	1	3
rags		1	1	room, operating	2	1	3
railing	3	4	7	room, pool	1		1
railroad	1		1	room, reception	1		1
rain	6	2	8	room, recitation	1		1
raincoat	1		1	room, recreation	1		1
raisins		1	1	room, school	1		1
ramp	2		2	room, shower		1	1
ranch	1		1	room, sitting	1		1
rapids	1		1	room, smoking		1	1
rat		1	1	room, stock	1		1
rattlesnake		1	1	room, sun		1	1
ravine	1	2	3	room, waiting		2	2
ray	1		1	room, wash	1		1
receptacle	1		1	rootbeer	1		1
record, phonograph	2	1	3	roots		1	1
residence	1		1	rope	2		2
resort	1	3	4	roses		2	2
restaurant	4	5	9	rubber	1	1	2
revolver	3		3	rubberbands		1	1
ribbon		5	5	rubies		1	1
rifle	5	1	6				
ring	4	15	19	sack	1		1
ring, boxing	1		1	salad	1	2	3

	M.	F.	B.		M.	F.	B.
saloon	1		1	ship	5	5	10
salt		1	1	shirt	5	10	15
sand	1	3	4	shoe	4	5	9
sand dune	1		1	shooting gallery	1		1
sandwiches	1	1	2	shop	9	3	12
sapphires	1		1	shore	2	4	6
sauerkraut	1		1	shorts	1	1	2
saw	1		1	shoulder	7	5	12
sawdust	1		1	shovel	1		1
scale	1		1	showcase	1		1
scarf		2	2	shrimp	1		1
school	13	34	47	shrubbery		2	2
school, grade		1	1	sidewalk	8	5	13
school, high	3	12	15	sign		3	3
school, jr. high		3	3	signal	2		2
school, medical	1		1	sill		1	1
school, Sunday		1	1	sink	1	2	3
schoolyard	1		1	siren	1	1	2
scissors	1	2	3	skates		1	1
score, musical		1	1	skin	2	1	3
scrapbook	1		1	skin, bear	1		1
screen	2		2	skirt	2	4	6
sea	3	1	4	ski jump		1	1
seal, animal		1	1	ski run	1		1
seal, official		1	1	skis	2		2
seashore	1		1	skull		1	1
seat	1		1	slab	1		1
seat cover	1		1	sled		2	2
seats	13	18	31	sleeves	2	1	3
seaweed		1	1	slide rule	1		1
sedative		1	1	slip, clothes		3	3
seed		1	1	slugs	1		1
semen	1		1	smoke	5	4	9
serum	1		1	snake	7	4	11
setting, jewel		1	1	snow	7	6	13
seven up		1	1	snowballs	1	1	2
sewing		1	1	soap	1	1	2
shacks	3		3	socket	1		1
shade	2	2	4	soda fountain		1	1
shadows		2	2	sofa	4		4
shaft	1		1	solution, cleaning		1	1
shavings		1	1	sores	2		2
sheaf	1		1	space, parking		1	1
shed	2		2	speedometer	1		1
sheep	1		1	spinal cord		1	1
sheet	4	3	7	spine		1	1
shelf	1	2	3	splinter		1	1
shell, gun	2		2	squirrel	1	1	2
shell, sea		1	1	stable		1	1
shelter		3	3	stack		1	1

	M.	F.	B.		M.	F.	B.
stadium	4	2	6	stump		1	1
stage	5	17	22	submarine		1	1
stairs	29	45	74	substation	1		1
stake	1		1	suburb	2	1	3
stalk	1		1	subway		1	1
stalls	1		1	suit	4	6	10
star	1	1	2	suit, bathing	2	3	5
State (specific)	12	12	24	suitcase	1	9	10
station	1	1	2	suite	3	7	10
station, bus		1	1	sun	5	7	12
station, gas	5		5	sundae	1		1
station, police	1		1	surf	1		1
station, radio	1		1	swamp	1	2	3
station, railroad	6	2	8	sweater	3	2	5
stationary		1	1	swing		1	1
statue	1		1	switch, light	3	1	4
steak		2	2	sword		1	1
steamer		1	1	syringe	1		1
steel	1		1				
stepladder		1	1				
sticks	1	2	3	table	24	30	54
stock		1	1	tackle, fishing	1		1
stockings	2	6	8	tadpoles		1	1
stomach	9	2	11	tag, price		1	1
stone	4	5	9	tail	1	1	2
stool	1	1	2	tank	2		2
store	16	25	41	tape	2		2
store, antique		1	1	target	1		1
store, book	2	1	3	tavern	3	1	4
store, clothing	2		2	taxi cab		1	1
store, department	2	2	4	tear, rip		1	1
store, drug	6	4	10	tears		3	3
store, fruit	1		1	teaspoon		1	1
store, furniture		1	1	teeth	7	13	20
store, grocery		1	1	telephone	2	6	8
store, jewelry	2		2	telephone book	1		1
store, shoe		1	1	telephone booth	1		1
stories, building	3	2	5	telephone wires	1		1
stove	1	1	2	television	2		2
strap		1	1	temple, building		1	1
straw	1		1	temple, head		1	1
stream	1		1	tent	1		1
street	78	71	149	terrace		2	2
streetcar	3	8	11	terrain	1		1
string	5		5	territory	2		2
structure	3	1	4	theater	2	7	9
student union, building		1	1	theme	1	1	2
studio		2	2	thermometer		1	1
study room	1	1	2	threshold		1	1
				throat	1	1	2

	M.	F.	B.		M.	F.	B.
throne	1	1	2	uniform	12	3	15
throttle		1	1	University (specific)	11	7	18
thumb	1		1	upstairs	4	13	17
ticket	4	6	10	uptown	1		1
tie	1	4	5	urethra	1		1
tiger	1	1	2				
tile		1	1	vagina	4		4
timberland	1		1	valise	1		1
tires	4		4	valley	2	2	4
toast		1	1	vases	1	2	3
tobacco	1		1	vault		1	1
toes		2	2	vegetables		1	1
tomatoes	1	1	2	vegetation		2	2
tomb	1		1	vehicles		1	1
tongue	1		1	veranda		1	1
tonic	1		1	vest	1		1
tonsils		1	1	vestibule		1	1
tools	1		1	village	1	1	2
toothbrush		1	1	violin	1	1	2
toothpaste	1		1	vulture		1	1
tornado	1	1	2				
towel	1	2	3	wagon		1	1
toy	1		1	waist	2	4	6
track, deer	1		1	walk, side	3	1	4
track, race	2		2	wall	9	19	28
track, railroad	4	1	5	wallet	1	1	2
track, streetcar	2	1	3	wallpaper		2	2
trail	2	1	3	ward		1	1
trailer	1		1	wash, laundry	1		1
train	8	7	15	washbowl	2		2
tray	1		1	washing machine		1	1
tree	17	10	27	wastebasket	1	2	3
tricycle		1	1	watch, timepiece		5	5
trigger	2		2	water	27	35	62
trimming		1	1	watertower	1		1
trousers	1	4	5	waves	2	4	6
truck	7	4	11	weapon	2	1	3
trunk	2		2	well	1		1
tub		1	1	wheel	3	1	4
tube	5		5	whip		1	1
tunnel	3	1	4	whirlpool		1	1
turbine	1		1	whiskers		3	3
turtle	1		1	whiskey	1		1
tusks	1		1	whistle	1	1	2
tuxedos	1	1	2	window	25	37	62
typewriter		2	2	windshield	1	1	
				wine		2	2
umbrella	1	2	3	wings	1	1	2
underbrush	1		1	wires,			
underclothes	4	2	6	communication	1		1

	M.	F.	B.		M.	F.	B.
wires, streetcar	1	1		yacht		1	1
wolf	2	2		yard	2	8	10
wood	2	6	8	yard, back	4	4	
wool		1	1	yard, railroad		1	1
worm		1	1	yard, school	1	1	
wreath		1	1	yearbook	1	1	
wreckage	1	1					
wrist	3	2	5	zipper	1	1	
writing		1	1	zone	1	1	

You Can Receive Books Like This One and Much, Much More

You can begin to receive books in the *A.R.E. Membership Series* and many more benefits by joining the non-profit Association for Research and Enlightenment, Inc., as a Sponsoring or Life member.

The A.R.E. has a worldwide membership that receives a wide variety of study aids, all aimed at assisting individuals in their spiritual, mental, and physical growth.

Every member of A.R.E. receives a copy of *Venture Inward*, the organization's bimonthly magazine; an in-depth journal, *The New Millennium* on alternate months; opportunity to borrow, through the mail, from a collection of more than 500 files on medical and metaphysical subjects; access to one of the world's most complete libraries on metaphysical and spiritual subjects; and opportunities to participate in conferences, international tours, a retreat-camp for children and adults, and numerous nationwide volunteer activities.

In addition to the foregoing benefits, Sponsoring and Life members also receive at no charge three books each year in the *A.R.E. Membership Series*.

If you are interested in finding out more about membership in A.R.E. and the many benefits that can assist you on your path to fulfillment, you can easily contact the Membership Department by writing Membership, A.R.E., P.O. Box 595, Virginia Beach, VA 23451-0595 or by calling **1-800-333-4499** or faxing **1-757-422-6921**.

**Explore our electronic visitor's center on the Internet:
http://www.are-cayce.com**